MW00453698

HOW TO BEAD EARRINGS:
An Artistic Approach

by

Lori S. Berry

Copyright © MCMXCIV by Eagle's View Publishing

All rights reserved. No part of this book may be reproduced or transmitted in any form or by any means, electronic or mechanical, including, but not restricted to, photocopying, recording, or using any information storage or retrieval system, without permission in writing from the publisher.

Eagle's View Publishing Company
6756 North Fork Road
Liberty, UT 84310

ISBN: 0-943604-34-6
Library of Congress Catalog Card Number: 93-70575

FIRST EDITION

10 9 8 7 6 5 4 3 2 1

TABLE OF CONTENTS

Getting Started 1
   Materials 1
   Using This Book 4
   Techniques 6

Flat Woven Earrings 11
   Comanche Stitch Earrings 11
   Non-Loom Stitch Earrings 23

Cabochon Earrings 33

How To Bead Crystals 39
   Beading Cylindrical Crystals 39
   Beading Spherical Crystals 46
   Beading Fluorite Crystals 53

Five New Beaded Earring Techniques 59
   Beaded Stars 59
   Beaded Hearts 63
   Beaded Feathers 67
   Beaded Flowers 73
   Beaded Rosettes 88

ABOUT THE AUTHOR

Lori has always been interested in Native American culture, and nine years ago she started studying beadwork— melding her art training with instruction learned from books and Indian craft classes. Since that time she has taught beadworking techniques to many people and has had her work exhibited and sold throughout the United States. Her earrings have also appeared in *The New Beadwork*, a book highlighting current beadwork artisans.

Lori lives with her husband and three daughters in San Pablo, California. Her original designs sell under the business name "Spotted Pony" and are in constant demand. Her jewelry has been the source of many open doors and new friendships.

ACKNOWLEDGEMENTS

I would first like to thank my husband Gene, who suggested that I write this book and continued to help and encourage me while taking care of home and family. Thanks also go to my "adopted Mom", Nina Berry, for her help and suggestions; to Alice Scherer, Director of the Center for the Study of Beadwork in Portland, Oregon, who always had an accurate and interesting answer for all my questions; and to my editor, Denise Knight, whose patient and practiced eye made this book the finished work that it is. Finally, thanks to my publisher, Monte Smith, who saw the merits of this book from the few rough pages I sent to him last year.

This book is dedicated to all my students, to all the beadworkers who have come before, and to you the reader—whose interest in the art of beadwork and hunger to expand the boundaries of design and technique, keeps the craft alive and growing.

In loving memory of my mother, Shirleey Katz, and my dear friend Mark Crissey, and in thanks to the inspiration from the One Above.

There are many great books on the market that show beadwork techniques and/or patterns. I collect all of them that I can find, but worth mentioning here are those which I have referred to in writing this book.

Aikman, Z. Susanne. *A Primer: The Art of Native American Beadwork.* Denver, Colorado: Morning Flower Press, 1980.

DeLange, Deon. *Techniques of Beading Earrings.* Liberty, Utah: Eagle's View Publishing Company, 1983.

_____. *More Techniques of Beading Earrings.* Liberty, Utah: Eagle's View Publishing Company, 1985.

Goodhue, Horace. *Indian Bead Weaving Patterns.* St. Paul, Minnesota: Bead-Craft, 1984.

Lyford, Carrie A. *Quill and Beadwork of the Western Sioux.* Boulder, Colorado: Johnson Books, 1979.

Spears, Therese. *Beaded Earrings.* Boulder, Colorado: Promenade, 1984.

GETTING STARTED

This book is intended to be interesting and challenging for both the beginner and the advanced beadwork artist. It begins with the Comanche (or Brick) and Non-Loom Stitches, which are easy and very popular methods of making earrings. The patterns provided for these stitches are unique and eye-catching; very different from the standard geometric designs which most books provide. This is followed by a basic chapter on beading around Cabochons (a simple way to make stunning earrings). The section on Beading Crystals provides a wide variety of earring styles, from the simple to the complex. Finally, the book shows how to create five new styles of earrings, again ranging from quick and easy styles to those which offer a challenge to the advanced beadworker. While the book provides patterns and explicit instructions, with plenty of illustrations, it is hoped that it will also encourage the reader to be creative and produce patterns and styles of their own.

MATERIALS

Before jumping into beadworking techniques, it is helpful to become familiar with the materials and tools used to make earrings. Much of this information is intended for the novice, but experienced beadworkers may find some interesting ideas as well.

Beads: Most of the beads used in this book are made from glass. Today, the major manufacturers of glass beads are Czechoslovakia, Japan, France and Taiwan. There are many opinions on which beads are the best to use, however, beads from any of these countries can be used to make beautiful earrings. The important thing is to sort the beads carefully and use only those which are uniform in size and shape. Generally, the quality of the beads is reflected in their price, and the trade off is between time spent sorting and money spent for more uniform beads.

Two main kinds of beads are used in the earrings in this book— seed beads and bugle beads. Seed beads have an oblong shape and come in several styles. Most of the seed beads used in this book are of the smooth or tumbled variety. Cut seed beads have small flat areas, or facets, on the surface of the bead which reflect light. Their edges are sometimes sharp and can cut beading thread, so be careful working with these. Bugle beads are small tubes of glass. The tube may be smooth, twisted or faceted. These beads are not polished and can also have sharp or chipped edges.

The different kinds of glass used to make beads transmit varying amounts of light. The main categories of bead glass are <u>transparent</u>, which is completely see through, and <u>opaque</u>, which can not be seen through at all.

Bead surfaces are also treated in a variety of ways to alter their appearance. Some of the common styles and a brief description are listed here. The comments provided are not intended to discourage the use of these beads; rather, they are a warning to be judicious about how and where these beads are used: <u>iridescent</u>, <u>iris</u> or <u>aurora borealis</u>— colors with a rainbow appearance; <u>pearl</u> or <u>Ceylon</u>— colors with a lustrous, pearl-like finish; <u>metallic</u> or <u>younie</u>— beads with a metallic finish which wears off with repeated handling; <u>painted</u> or <u>dyed</u>— beads dipped in a coloring substance, (a delicate finish which will fade with extended exposure to light and which will rub off); <u>color-lined</u>— transparent beads with a different color painted in their holes (this lining may deteriorate with excessive wear on the holes and will also fade with extended light exposure); and <u>rocaille</u> or <u>silver-lined</u>— beads lined with a silver or gold material (this lining may wear off or tarnish over time). Most bugle beads are of the rocaille variety.

Seed beads range in size from 5/° (pronounced five-ought) to 24/°. The smaller the number, the larger the bead. Generally, the bead sizes recommended in this book will be 11/° and 13/°, because these sizes are easy to find and are available in a wide range of colors. Size 12/° 3-cut beads are suggested in some places for added sparkle and shine; 12/° 3-cuts or 14/° hexagon beads may be substituted for 13/° beads in any pattern. Be aware that all countries manufacture their beads in characteristic ways and that, in addition to differences in uniformity and shape, there are differences in size. A good rule is— don't trust the labeled size of any bead. Take along any beads already bought and compare them to the ones being considered.

Bugle beads may be labeled with a size number (up to 5), the length in inches or the length in millimeters (mm). The following table provides approximate equivalents:

Size	mm	inches
#2	5	3/16
#3	7	1/4
#4	9	5/16
#5	11	3/8

In most cases, the shorter the bugle bead, the smaller the diameter. In woven work, the smaller size bugles (up to size 2) should be used in conjunction with size 12/° or smaller seed beads. Size 3, 4 or 5 bugle beads may be used with size 11/° seed beads. The larger bugles (15 mm and up) are mainly used as fringe beads, but can also be used with size 10/° or larger seed beads.

Beads are sold in various forms and quantities. They come on strings in bunches called "hanks", or loose in bags, tubes or plastic containers. Loose beads are sold by the ounce or partial ounce. Regardless of packaging, beads can be purchased by the kilo and a quantity discount is usually available. Always buy plenty of beads. Beads, like yarn and material, come in different manufactured lots, and the colors of one batch may not match the colors of another. Each type of bead is usually labeled or cataloged by the retailer with some kind of reference number. It is very helpful to write down the reference number, price and source of every bead purchased. This will aid in reordering and cataloging your bead supply.

Needles: Beading needles are primarily manufactured in England and Japan. The English needles are preferred by most beadworkers, because their eyes are narrower and they are sturdier. The Japanese needles are more flexible, but they break more easily.

Needles come in different lengths designed for different kinds of work. For beaded earrings, the short or "sharps" type of needle is best because it allows more maneuverability between beads. Regular beading needles can be useful for the Peyote Stitch, or when finishing-off thread ends that are extremely short.

Needle sizes indicate diameter and correspond roughly with bead sizes (although some beads have larger holes than others). The larger the number the thinner the needle. Generally, use a needle which is the same size or one size smaller than the seed beads used. If it becomes hard to push a needle through a bead, switch to a smaller needle to avoid breaking the bead. It is best to keep an assortment of needles on hand and to have a generous supply of the size(s) used most often. Size 15 and 16 needles can be hard to find and rather expensive, but they will prevent the loss of a project to a broken bead, saving much time and frustration.

Thread: The best and most often used thread for beading earrings is called "Nymo". This is a strong thread, made of parallel nylon filaments. It comes in several colors and is sold on bobbins, spools or large cones. Nymo does stretch, which is occasionally a problem, but one that is usually easy to correct.

Nymo comes in a variety of thicknesses or sizes. From thin to thick, these are: 000, 00, 0, A, B, C, D and F. Use the thickest, and therefore strongest, thread which will still fit through the beads the required number of times. With size 11/° beads, this will be size 0, A or B thread, depending on the complexity of the stitch; with size 13/° beads, use size 0 or A. Size B or C is good to use with size 11/° beads around cabochons or in beaded edgings, because these beads are subject to lots of stress and have relatively few threads through them.

Some people prefer polyester sewing thread, which comes in a multitude of colors, or Monocord, a nylon thread which resembles thin fishing line. For working on crystals, silk thread is ideal; it is a natural fiber, which will make the purists happy, and is much stronger than cotton thread. There is a new thread on the market called Kevlar, which is made from the same material as bullet proof vests. This thread is as thin as Nymo, comes in more colors (except white) and will not break or stretch.

Beeswax: Although some people would rather not bother, beeswax is an important tool. Waxing keeps the thread moving smoothly through the beads, helps prevent tangles and protects the thread from fraying. Just two or three passes over a cake of beeswax is all it takes.

Scissors: A small pair of sharp embroidery scissors is essential for clipping threads close to the beadwork, so that the ends will not show. A small pair of utility scissors should also be on hand for cutting material or beading wire.

Pliers: Another useful tool is a pair of needle-nosed pliers. These are used to attach findings to the finished earrings, and for pulling a needle through a tight bead. Be careful, because an overzealous person can wind up breaking the bead instead of coaxing the needle through.

Backing Material: Backing material is sometimes used to attach beadwork to crystals or to findings. Use lightweight suede leather or ultrasuede material in a neutral color or in a color that complements the earring design. If clear beads or cabochons are used, choose a white backing.

Glue: Glue is sometimes used to attach beadwork to backing materials, crystals or findings. Three types of glue are recommended: Barge Cement is good for tasks, such as gluing backing materials together, where a flexible, non-clear glue is needed; 527 Bond Cement is a flexible, clear glue which is ideal for holding diverse materials, such as leather, metal and glass, together; Super Glue forms a strong, inflexible bond, which is good for gluing on rigid surfaces such as crystals. Other types of glue are available and experimentation will determine personal preferences.

One or two drops are usually sufficient to adhere any two surfaces together. An excessive amount of glue will leak and may ruin the beadwork. Let any glued piece dry for at least 24 hours before handling (with the exception of Super Glue, which can be handled lightly within a few minutes).

When using any glue, work in a well ventilated area and follow the manufacturer's instructions for proper use. Make sure that all surfaces to be cemented are clean and be aware that some glues have the ability to fade or alter bead colors.

Clear Fingernail Polish: Clear nail polish is used to stiffen and hold the shape of non-moving portions of many earring styles, especially on areas which tend to curl.

Bead Containers/Storage: Beads can be stored in almost any container which can be securely closed, from ziplock bags to baby food jars. If the containers are transparent, it will be easier to identify the contents, but the beads should then be stored someplace dark (like a box or closet) so that their colors will not fade.

As the beads left over from projects expand into a collection, it becomes essential to devise a system of bead storage and organization. A large fishing tackle box is ideal because it can be carried or stored easily, is light resistant and contains plenty of different compartments. Another good system is a series of flat, compartmentalized tackle boxes with tight-fitting lids. There are also tackle containers that are a series of round interlocking plastic "jars". The author has two systems; a general storage system of plastic bags (divided by bead color and type) stored in boxes, and a portable system with a selection of beads stored in the interlocking tackle jars and carried in a small briefcase.

Dentalium Shells: These are small conical sea shells which make an interesting addition to the fringe portion of an earring. They come in small and large sizes, and should be soaked in mild soap and water and cleaned before use. If the shells are plugged with sand and grit, remove it by poking a size 12 or larger needle through both ends until the passage is clear. Also, the narrow end may not have a hole in it, or the hole may be too small. Remedy this by taking a small pair of utility scissors (not the good embroidery scissors) and cutting off small portions of this end.

Porcupine Quills: These make another unusual addition to earring fringe. They are light in color with a dark tip and the center is filled with a soft pith, which is easily removed. It is sometimes possible to find quills that have been cleaned and dyed different colors. Undyed quills should be cleaned by soaking them in warm soapy water for about 10 minutes and then rinsing them in a colander. Place them on a towel to dry. (Be careful of the black tips; they are barbed, sharp and dangerous!) Trim just enough off each end to allow a needle to pass through without splitting the quill. Then take a long sewing needle or pin (something which is larger in diameter than a beading needle) and run it through the pith in the center portion of the quill. Stay in the middle of the quill; if the needle hits the outer edges, it will leave a translucent scrape mark which is visible on the outside of the quill.

When choosing quills for an earring, sort out several which are similar in length and diameter (some quills will be thicker than others). With the black tips towards the top, line up the bottoms of the dark portions on a cutting board. Use a knife to cut the white portions to the length desired for the earring. This method insures the quills will all be the same length. String the quills with the dark tip pointing towards the bottom of the fringe. Quills must be handled and stored carefully, because they are very fragile and will bend or break easily. The best method of storage is a baby food jar or other rigid container.

Porcupine quills are regulated or even illegal in some states, so check on local laws before purchasing or using them.

Findings: The jewelry hardware used to attach earrings to ears are called findings. The earrings in this book mostly call for one of the several different styles of ear wires, ear hooks or earring posts made for pierced ears (Figure 1-1). The "best" style to use depends somewhat on the type of earring, and even more on the personal preferences of the person who will wear it. Findings made for non-pierced ears usually clip or screw onto the ear and can also be used.

Figure 1-1

For findings with ring attachment points, always twist the ring open sideways, slip the earring loop into the ring, then twist the ring closed (Figure 1-2). Do <u>not</u> pull the ends of the ring apart or they will not align properly when the ring is again closed.

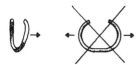

Figure 1-2

Sources: Most of these materials are available from bead supply stores, trading posts, general craft stores and Indian craft stores. Don't discount the possibility of purchasing supplies by mail order, as this increases the selection of materials available. Gem and crystal shows are great places to find unique items, such as crystals, cabochons and handcrafted findings, as well as beads. Whatever the source, look the merchandise over carefully and ask lots of questions.

USING THIS BOOK

To get the most out of this book, everyone should read *Getting Started,* then leaf through the book to choose a project. The techniques presented in this book build upon one another, with the easiest techniques preceding the more difficult ones. Each new technique utilizes preceding methods and while the locations of earlier instructions are referenced, only new procedures are fully explained and illustrated.

Therefore, the first step is to read through the chosen project completely. Visualize each procedure, from beginning to end, and locate and review any previously-described methods which are not familiar. The bead numbering system used in the text and illustrations follows the order in which the beads are added to the beadwork. For complicated techniques, beads are identified with both a number and a letter; the numbers indicate the row and the letters indicate the sequence of the beads within that row; thus bead #2a is the first bead in the second row.

One or more patterns follow the instructions for each technique. Often, variations which alter the look or design of the earring are also suggested and explained. Since many of the patterns are asymmetrical, the second earring of each pair should be flipped over before the finding is attached, so that the earring designs mirror one another when worn (Figure 1-3).

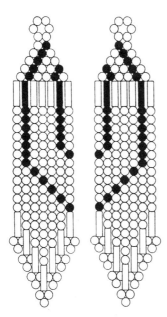

Figure 1-3

The patterns provided in this book offer suggested colors, but they are intended to open each reader's mind to new possibilities in beadworking. After beading each pattern, try experimenting with different colors to personalize the earrings, then try creating new patterns.

There are some color combinations which seem to work very well together; pink and purple, red and white, gold and red, blue and yellow, and black with anything. The best way to experiment is to start lining up different colors of beads next to one another to see what combinations are pleasing.

It is important to note that when designing earrings, the colors used must be distinctively different from one another. Two beads of different shades of the same color may look different when viewed separately, but when the colors are strung together, they may look about the same.

When choosing beads for cabochon or crystal projects, make sure and use colors that match or complement the item to be beaded. When selecting fringe materials, utilize beads that correspond to the colors and designs within the base earring.

To encourage original designs, blank bead graphs are provided. Figure 1-4 can be used for charting fringe and Non-Loom Stitch designs, Figure 1-5 for charting Comanche Stitch designs, and Figure 1-6 for charting Peyote Stitch designs.

Figure 1-4

Figure 1-5

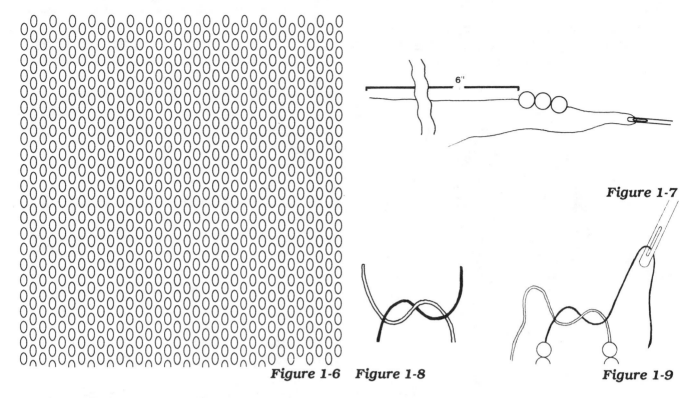

Figure 1-7

Figure 1-6   Figure 1-8   Figure 1-9

TECHNIQUES

Beading Surfaces and Environment:
Always bead on a rough surface, such as a towel or fabric-covered piece of foam, to prevent beads and supplies from rolling or sliding away. While beading, beads can be piled by type on such a surface, or shallow containers can be used to hold the different types of beads. Individual saucers or jar lids, microwave dinner trays, a cafeteria tray or a paint palette are a few of the choices. Both the beading surface and containers should be white, or a neutral color such as beige, to allow maximum visibility for inspecting bead color and shape. Choose a comfortable chair and make sure the beading surface is at a comfortable height.

A well-lit area is also important; improper lighting can cause eye strain. Non-fluorescent lighting is best, as this does not alter the appearance of the bead colors. An excellent piece of equipment is a combination light and magnifying glass; this gives tired or farsighted eyes a good close look at knots in thread or imperfections in beads.

Bead Selection: While making earrings, both seed and bugle beads should be sorted for evenness of size, shape and color. Every batch will have some beads which are irregular in shape or which vary from the average size. Using these beads in the body of the beadwork will cause the earrings to appear uneven and sloppy. However, many of the rejected beads can be used elsewhere. Perfectly sized beads are not necessary for the "bottom beads" which secure the ends of fringe segments, and at some point in its construction an earring may require a thicker or thinner bead to properly fill a space.

Another good use for discarded beads is on bead inventory cards. Divide the rejects by color, size and style. Use pieces of heavy weight cardboard cut to fit into a ring binder, or 4" x 5" blank index cards which can be inserted into plastic photo-holder pages and then placed in a ring binder. Use separate sheets or cards for each color bead. Thread size C or larger Nymo thread on a size 12 needle and knot one end. Push the needle through the cardboard, string five or six of the same bead in a vertical line and go through the cardboard again. Skip over 1/2 inch or so and string the next style or size of bead. Leave plenty of space between the vertical lines, so that more bead samples can be added in the future. Leave room on the bottom of each line of beads to write down their reference number, price and the store where they were purchased.

Thread: Unless otherwise specified, a single thread, unknotted at both ends, is used to make the earrings in this book. A "hanging" thread of about six inches should be left below the first bead strung, to be knotted and hidden when the beadwork is completed (Figure 1-7). The "main" thread is the thread attached to the needle and used to add new beads. Once a thread has been knotted or tied off, it is called a thread end.

Avoid working with more thread than is comfortable; an excess amount of thread can get tangled or knotted and more thread can always be added, if needed, to finish an earring. Thread lengths are suggested for each technique, but be aware that if a variation uses more beads than in the basic instructions, more thread will be required to complete the project.

Knotting Thread: To complete an earring, the excess thread on either end must be tied off or knotted. The four knots used in this book are: an overhand knot tied by hand (Figure 1-8); an overhand knot tied with a needle (Figure 1-9); a square knot (Figure 1-10); and a backstitch knot (Figure 1-11). In some places, repetitions (e.g., 2 overhand knots) or combinations of these knots (e.g., a square knot with an overhand knot on top of it) will be specified.

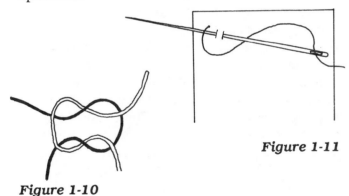

Figure 1-11

Figure 1-10

Adding Thread: Sometimes thread must be added to complete a project. One method is to leave about six inches on the end of the old thread, to which the extra thread can be added, and remove the needle. Cut and wax enough extra thread to finish the work and thread it onto the needle. Leave a new hanging thread and tie the two thread ends together with a square knot. Maneuver the knot as close as possible to the last bead on the piece (Figure 1-12); if necessary, insert the needle into the center of the square knot and push the knot over to the bead. When the knot is in position, tie an overhand knot to keep it from sliding and

continue constructing the earring in the normal manner.

Another method of adding thread is to knot off the thread when there is about six inches remaining and remove the needle. Cut and wax a new piece of thread, put it on the needle and push the needle under the thread of a previously stitched part of the work. Leave a new hanging thread and tie a square knot around the thread in the completed portion of the beadwork. Weave through the beadwork to the new starting point and continue constructing the earring in the normal manner (Figure 1-13).

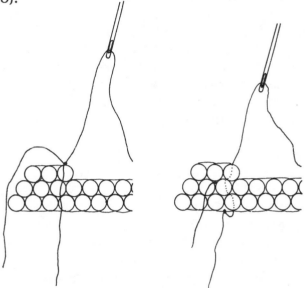

Figure 1-12   *Figure 1-13*

When the work is finished, hide all the thread ends (new and old) by weaving them into the beadwork as described for each beading technique.

Cutting Thread From Finished Beadwork: The best way to cut excess thread from a finished project is to hold the scissors flat against (parallel to) the beadwork. Pull the

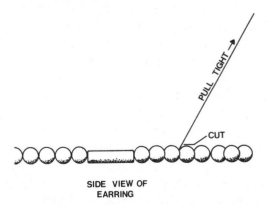

SIDE VIEW OF EARRING

Figure 1-14

thread away from the earring at a right angle to the scissors, maintaining a tight tension on the thread. Push the scissors down, as close to the bead from which the thread protrudes as possible, and carefully clip the thread (Figure 1-14). Failure to keep the scissors and beadwork parallel to one another can result in cutting into the beadwork.

Finishing Touches: To stiffen and hold the shape of non-moving portions of an earring, apply clear fingernail polish to the back side of the earring. Be sure to test the nail polish on some extra or reject beads before applying it to an earring; nail polish contains acetone, which can melt plastic beads or remove the color from painted, dyed and color-lined beads.

Put the earrings, face down, on a piece of wax paper and apply a thin coat of nail polish to the back side of the earring. Let it dry for about two hours and apply a second coat, if desired, for added strength. If the earring has fringe, take extra care and avoid getting any polish on the fringe portion; polish on the fringe will prevent it from swinging freely.

Fringe: Fringe is the free-swinging portion of an earring which is strung from the bottom of the base row; it can be a series of single, straight elements, a series of looped elements or a mixture of both.

Straight fringe elements are strung beneath each bead in the base row. They are started by running the needle down through the first bead and stringing the beads for that element on the thread. Usually there is a bugle bead or porcupine quill near the end, followed by one or more bottom beads to hold the fringe beads in position. The needle is brought back up through the bugle bead, the fringe beads above it, and the bottom row bead from which the element originated (Figure 1-15).

Looped fringe is started in the same way as straight fringe, however, instead of ending with a bugle bead and bottom beads, the fringe elements are repeated in reverse order. The end of the element is then attached to the base row bead at the opposite end of the earring by bringing the needle up through the bottom of this bead. Subsequent loops are strung inward, between the two base row beads just inside the last loop (Figure 1-16). After all the loops are strung, reinforce the loop elements by going through them again with the needle and thread.

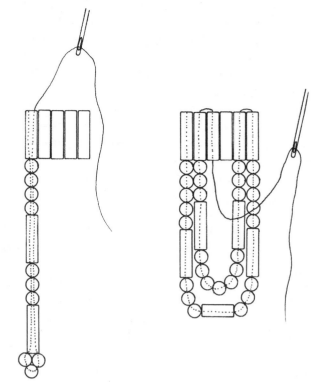

Figure 1-15   *Figure 1-16*

Fringe Tension: Fringe tension is one of the most important skills to master in making an attractive earring. After bringing the needle back up through the base row bead, pull the thread through the fringe element snug, but not too tight. A good rule is to leave a space between the fringe beads and the base beads which is about the thickness of a fingernail. The aim is to have the fringe swing freely as the earring moves when worn. The tension on any of the fringe segments can always be adjusted until the thread is knotted to finish the earring. If the tension is too tight on the first fringe segment, tug on the last fringe segment strung to get an excess amount of thread. Then tug on the next to the last segment, and so on towards the first segment, until the tension is adjusted correctly. The tension in each fringe segment affects the tension in all the others; if one is adjusted, the two next to it will be most directly affected. Experiment a bit with the fringe on the first earring to become familiar with how to properly adjust the tension.

Fringe Design and Materials: In most of the Comanche and Non-Loom patterns provided, the fringe design is a continuation of the design within the woven portion of the earring. The fringe, however, need not function solely in this manner. Fringe can serve as a counterpoint to the design, using materials not found in the main portion of the earring, or a simple main pattern can be devised and the fringe can become the focus of the earring by using materials such as large glass, plastic, clay or mineral beads. An infinite variety of these beads is available, just select sizes and colors which will harmonize with the main design. Some ideas are illustrated in Figure 1-17. Don't forget to use other materials, such as porcupine quills and dentalium shells, within fringe elements.

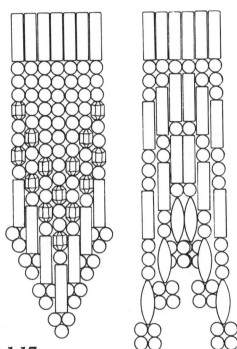

Figure 1-17

The overall shape of the fringe itself may also be varied. Figure 1-18 shows several different fringe shape designs. Even the bottom beads which hold each fringe segment in place have unlimited design alternatives. Some suggestions are shown in Figure 1-19.

Making Drop Earrings: Most of the smaller earrings in this book can be adapted into hanging or drop earrings by attaching them to the bottom of a single fringe segment. Several of these drop elements can be hung from a single attachment loop to create yet another look.

Drop earrings can be constructed in two ways; the small earring elements can be beaded separately and attached when the fringe and loop portions are made, or the fringe and earring elements can be made as one piece. If the earring elements take more than five feet of thread apiece, consider beading them separately.

For separate elements, bead the main earring portions completely, including an attachment loop. Then determine the amount of thread needed for the drop fringe segments, including an attachment loop at the top, bottom loops, and enough thread to hide the thread ends. String the beads for the attachment loop of the drop fringe first, leaving a hanging thread. Knot the main and hanging threads at the base of this loop (Figure 1-20).

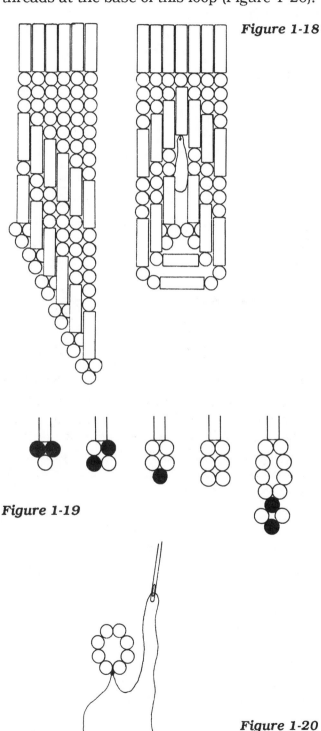

Figure 1-18

Figure 1-19

Figure 1-20

String the beads for the first fringe seg-

9

ment, then add six to eight beads for a bottom loop. Run the beads for the bottom loop through the attachment loop of the first main earring element (Figure 1-21). Reinforce the bottom loop by running the needle through all the bottom loop beads again. Adjust the tension in the fringe segment at this time. Go up through the fringe segment beads to the hanging thread and back through the beads in the attachment loop of the drop fringe. Exit by the hanging thread. If there is only one drop element, tie the main and hanging threads together and hide the ends in the fringe segment (Figure 1-22).

To construct a drop earring in one piece, allow enough thread for both the fringe segments and all the main earring elements that will be beaded. Start with the attachment loop for the drop element and then string the beads for the first fringe segment, as described for the separate attachment technique. No bottom loop is required. Bead the main earring element in the normal manner, paying close attention to the fringe tension (Figure 1-23), but do not bead an attachment loop on this main earring piece. Instead, thread the needle back to the top of the main earring piece and go back up through the fringe segment beads and through the beads of the attachment loop for the drop element. Exit by the hanging thread.

If beading more than one drop element, continue by repeating the procedure just described (Figure 1-24). Finish the earring in the manner described for the drop earrings with separately beaded elements.

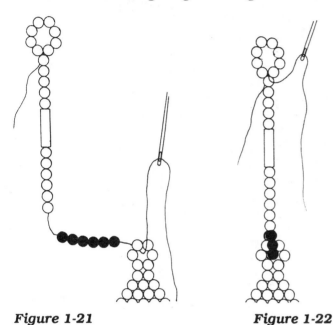

Figure 1-21   *Figure 1-22*

To add more drop elements, string the second set of fringe beads after exiting by the hanging thread. Make the second fringe segment longer or shorter than the first one. Repeat the technique described for the first drop element.

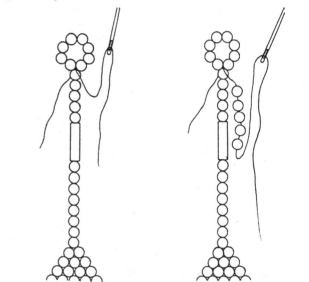

Figure 1-23   *Figure 1-24*

FLAT WOVEN EARRINGS

Most beaded earrings are made by stringing beads onto a single needle and thread and then weaving the thread through the beads to connect them in various ways. The most familiar techniques weave the beads together in a flat, two-dimensional form. This section contains instructions for two of the easiest methods for creating flat woven earrings.

COMANCHE STITCH EARRINGS

Suggested Materials:

Size A or Size B Nymo Thread
Size 13 and Size 15 Beading Needles
Size 11/° Seed Beads
Size 3 and Size 4 Bugle Beads
Fringe Materials as Desired

The Comanche Stitch (also known as the Brick Stitch) is the stitch most commonly used to make beaded earrings. It features a triangular top with a beaded, free swinging fringe.

Four Bugle Bead Base - Pattern A

In Pattern A, as shown in the legend, the bugle beads and the seed beads marked with diagonal lines are pink, and the cross-hatched beads are purple. To aid the beginner in understanding patterns, bead colors will be used in this first set of instructions. Follow the pattern while reading these instructions so that the other patterns in this book will be more readily understood. Do not hesitate to try other color combinations; the possibilities are endless on a simple pattern such as this one. Other suggestions are black and white, gold and green, and dark and light blue.

The stitch used to make the base row of this earring is called the Ladder Stitch. This row anchors both the Comanche Stitch rows above it and the fringe segments that hang below it. To start this row, thread a size 13 needle with approximately 1-1/2 feet of waxed Nymo thread. Reserve the size 15 needles in case it becomes difficult to push a size 13

needle through a seed or bugle bead with several strands of thread already through it. Hold the long end of the thread and string two bugle beads (#1-#2) over the needle. Slide them down to about six inches from the end (Figure 2-1). Leave this end of the thread "hanging"; it will be tied off when the earring is completed.

Bring the needle back up through the bottom of bugle bead #1 (Figure 2-2), and pull these beads together and parallel while holding onto bugle bead #1. Do not pull too tight, as this will pull out the hanging thread. Keep the hanging thread on the bottom left side of the bugle bead base.

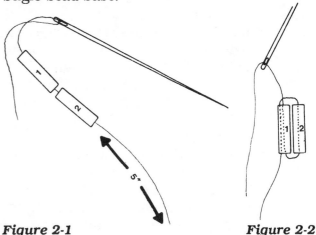

Figure 2-1   Figure 2-2

11

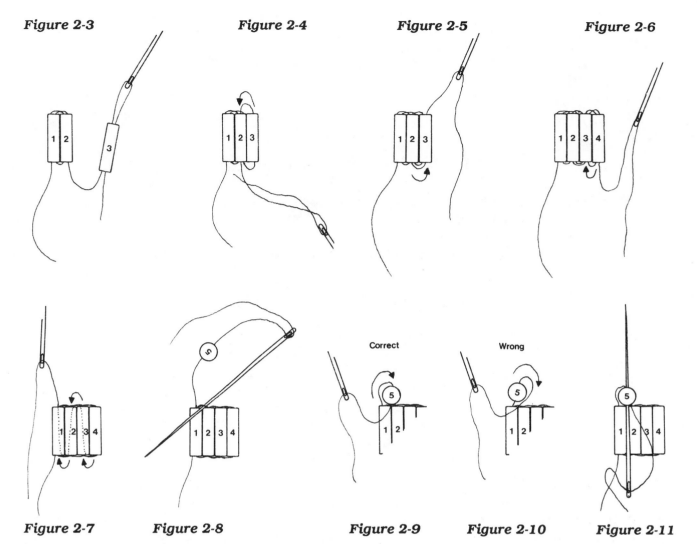

Figure 2-7   Figure 2-8   Figure 2-9   Figure 2-10   Figure 2-11

Now bring the needle back down through the top of bugle bead #2. Pull the first two beads together and string another bugle bead (#3) on the thread (Figure 2-3). Bring the needle down through the top of bugle bead #2 (Figure 2-4), pull the thread tight and put the needle up through the bottom of bugle bead #3 (Figure 2-5).

To attach the last bead of this row, string a bugle bead (#4) and bring the needle up through the bottom of bugle bead #3. Pull the thread tight until bead #4 snaps into place next to bugle bead #3 and put the needle down through the top of bugle bead #4 (Figure 2-6).

Put the needle up through the bottom of bugle bead #3, down through the top of bugle bead #2, and up through the bottom of bugle bead #1 (Figure 2-7). All the bugle beads should be strung tightly against one another with no gaps between them. If this base is too loose, snip the thread and start again.

To begin the actual Comanche Stitch, string a purple seed bead (#5) and bring the

needle under the thread between bugle beads #1 and #2, from behind the bugle beads towards the front (Figure 2-8). Pull the thread through until the seed bead rests snugly on top of the bugle beads.

This bead (#5) will tend to sit one of two ways on top of the bugle beads. The objective is to keep the thread on the outside of the bead, with the bead resting between the first two bugle beads. To do this, push the bead towards the center of the earring (Figure 2-9). If the bead is on the outside of the first bugle bead, with the thread to the inside of the bead (Figure 2-10), simply flip the bead over.

When the bead is seated properly, bring the needle back up through the bottom of bead #5, staying on the front side of the bugles (Figure 2-11). Do <u>not</u> allow the needle to go under the threads connecting the bugle beads while pushing the needle through the seed bead; this will cause the seed bead to come off the thread.

Now string a pink seed bead (#6) onto the

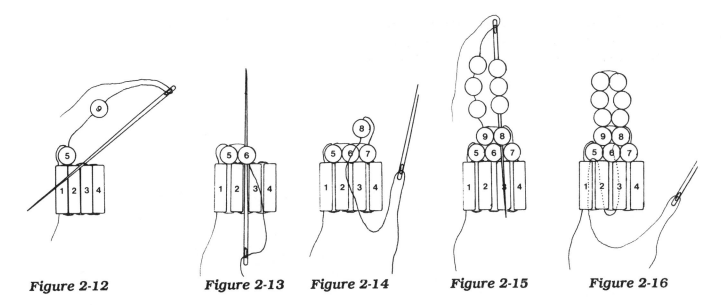

| Figure 2-12 | Figure 2-13 | Figure 2-14 | Figure 2-15 | Figure 2-16 |

thread and again bring the needle from behind the bugles, under the thread between bugle beads #2 and #3 (Figure 2-12). Put the needle up through the bottom of seed bead #6 (Figure 2-13). Next, string a purple seed bead (#7) and use the same procedure to attach it between bugle beads #3 and #4. This is the last bead of this row.

The direction of bead stringing for the second row is from right to left. To start, string a purple bead (#8) and put the needle under the threads between beads #6 and #7 in the previous row (Figure 2-14). Make sure the thread is on the outside of bead #8, as was done at the start of the first row. Bring the needle back up through bead #8. Pull the thread snug, but not too tight or the beads will buckle; if the thread is too loose, the earring will look like a beaded fish net. String another purple bead (#9) and anchor it to the threads between beads #5 and #6 with the Comanche Stitch technique.

Make an attachment loop by stringing six pink beads onto the thread and pushing the needle down through the top of bead #8 (Figure 2-15).

To position the thread for adding the fringe segments, push the needle down through the top of bead #6; down through the top of bugle bead #3; up through the bottom of bugle bead #2; and down through the top of bugle bead #1 (Figure 2-16). The hanging and main threads are now coming out of the same bugle bead.

String the first set of fringe beads—two purple seed beads, one pink bugle bead, three purple seed beads, one pink seed bead, one purple seed bead, three pink seed beads and one pink bugle bead. The next beads to be strung ("bottom beads") will secure the end of the fringe and allow the continued stringing of fringe bead segments. Use one purple, one pink and one purple bead.

Hold the bottom beads in one hand and push the needle back up through the fringe beads; then go up through the bottom of bugle bead #1 (Figure 2-17). Pull the thread snug, but not too tight (see the section on adjusting fringe tension in *Getting Started*).

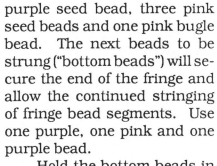

Figure 2-17

Now push the needle down through the top of bugle bead #2, ready to string the second fringe segment. Don't tug the thread too hard or it will upset the tension on the first fringe segment. Continue to follow Pattern A using the same fringe attachment technique outlined above. Notice that the color and placement of the beads will be different.

When the last fringe segment has been strung, knot off and finish the earring. The needle and thread should be coming out of the top of bugle bead #4. Push the needle up through seed beads #7 and #8, and counterclockwise through all the attachment loop beads. Then push the needle down through the top of seed bead #9 and exit out the bottom of seed

13

bead #5 (Figure 2-18). Finally, make two over-hand knots around the thread between bugle beads #1 and #2 (Figure 2-19; the beads in this Figure are separated for illustrative purposes only).

Figure 2-18

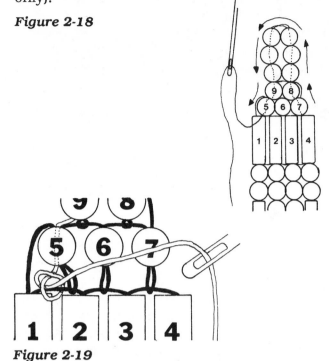

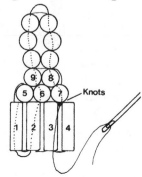

Figure 2-19

To hide this main thread, push the needle down through the top of bugle bead #2, up through the bottom of bugle bead #3, and then up through the bottom of seed bead #6. Cut this thread carefully, remembering to keep the scissors flat against the beadwork.

To knot and hide the hanging thread, thread it on the needle and push the needle up through the bottoms of beads #2, #6 and #9; go clockwise through all the attachment loop beads, and then down through the tops of seed beads #8 and #7. Make two overhand knots around the thread between bugle beads #3 and #4 (Figure 2-20). Push the needle down through the top of bugle bead #3, up through the bottom of bugle bead #2, and then up through the bottom of seed bead #6. Cut this thread and attach a finding to the earring.

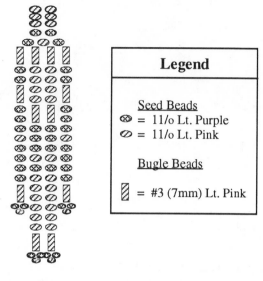

Figure 2-20

Pattern A

Legend
Seed Beads
⊗ = 11/o Lt. Purple
⊘ = 11/o Lt. Pink
Bugle Beads
▨ = #3 (7mm) Lt. Pink

Seven Bugle Bead Base - Pattern B

The base row of Comanche Stitch earrings can be made with an odd number of beads as opposed to the even number in Pattern A. There are slight differences between even and odd-numbered base row earrings. First, the more beads there are in the base row, the more beads there are in the top portion of the earring. Each additional bead in the base row increases the number of rows in the top portion by one; e.g., if there are four beads in the base row, there will be two rows in the top portion; if there are five beads in the base row, there will be three rows in the top portion, etc.

The only other difference between even and odd-numbered base rows is that the attachment loop is started from different sides. In an even-numbered base row earring, the attachment loop is started from the left side. Conversely, in an odd-numbered base row earring, the attachment loop is started from the right side.

Pattern B illustrates how to work with more beads in the top rows, and how to work with an odd-numbered base row earring. Thread a size 13 needle with a waxed piece of Nymo thread approximately 3 feet long. Follow the directions for making a bugle bead base given for the earrings in Pattern A. After bugle bead #4, keep stringing bugle beads, using the Ladder Stitch technique, until bugle bead #7 has been strung on the needle. Then weave the thread up and down through the bugle beads, exiting from the top of bugle bead #1. From here on the instructions for implementing the Comanche Stitch are the same as for the earrings in Pattern A. Only the number of beads in each row and the number of rows are different.

Follow Pattern B for bead and color placement, and when ready to add the attachment loop, notice that the needle will be coming out of bead #27, on the right (Figure 2-21). String six attachment loop beads and push the needle down into the top of seed beads #26, #25, #19, #18 and #8, and then down through the top of bugle bead #1 (Figure 2-22). As in Pattern A, the main and hanging thread are extending out of the bottom of the same bugle bead.

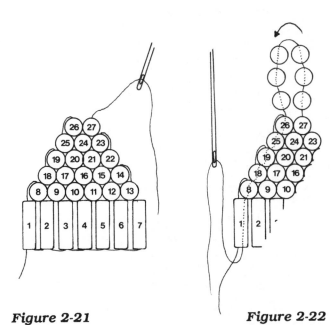

Figure 2-21   **Figure 2-22**

To construct the fringe portion, follow Pattern B again as to bead and color placement. When all the fringe segments have been strung, the needle will be coming out the top of bugle bead #7 (Figure 2-23).

To reinforce the attachment loop, push the needle up through seed beads #13, #14, #22, #23 and #27, go counterclockwise through the six attachment loop beads, and back down through seed beads #26, #24, #21, #15 and #12. Tie two overhand knots around the thread between bugle beads #5 and #6 (Figure 2-24). To hide this thread, push the needle back up through seed beads #12, #15, #21 and #24. Cut the main thread after it has passed through bead #24.

Now thread the needle with the hanging thread, push it up through the bottom of bugle bead #2 and up through the bottom of seed

beads #8, #18, #19, #25 and #26. Go clockwise through the attachment loop beads and back down through seed beads #27, #24, #20, #17 and #9. Tie two overhand knots around the thread between bugle beads #2 and #3, and hide this thread back up through the bottom of seed beads #9, #17, #20 and #24. When finished hiding this thread, cut it carefully.

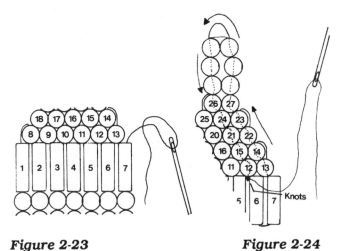

Figure 2-23   **Figure 2-24**

When both earrings are completed, flip one so that the rainbow designs face each other before attaching the ear wires.

Pattern B: Rainbow

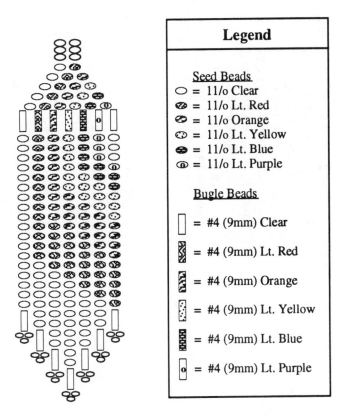

Legend
Seed Beads
○ = 11/o Clear
⊗ = 11/o Lt. Red
⊘ = 11/o Orange
⊙ = 11/o Lt. Yellow
⊛ = 11/o Lt. Blue
⊕ = 11/o Lt. Purple
Bugle Beads
▯ = #4 (9mm) Clear
▨ = #4 (9mm) Lt. Red
▤ = #4 (9mm) Orange
▢ = #4 (9mm) Lt. Yellow
▦ = #4 (9mm) Lt. Blue
▯ = #4 (9mm) Lt. Purple

15

Seed Bead Base - Patterns C to H

The base row can also be made with seed beads instead of bugle beads. Six patterns using seed beads in the base row of the earring are provided. Each pattern lists suggested materials and colors, but don't be afraid to personalize the designs by using different colors or substituting fringe materials.

The instructions for making earrings with a seed bead base instead of a bugle bead base are exactly the same as for Patterns A and B. Just be more patient and careful when holding and stringing the beads together with the Ladder Stitch in the base row. With a little practice it will become just as easy as using bugle beads. Remember that each additional row of seed beads requires the use of more thread.

Pattern C: Peacock

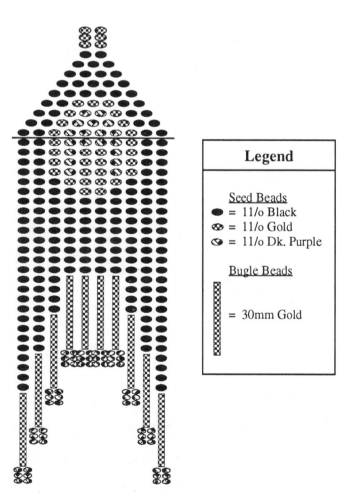

Legend

Seed Beads
● = 11/o Black
❀ = 11/o Gold
❂ = 11/o Dk. Purple

Bugle Beads

▦ = 30mm Gold

Pattern D: Navajo

Legend

Seed Beads
◓ = 11/o Turquoise
◒ = 11/o Peach
◑ = 11/o Pearl Purple
◍ = 11/o Pearl Pink
⊕ = 11/o Pearl Beige
❀ = 11/o Silver

Bugle Beads

▩ = #3 (7mm) Lt. Purple

▨ = #3 (7mm) Silver

▨ = #5 (11mm) Silver

16

Pattern E: Pegasus

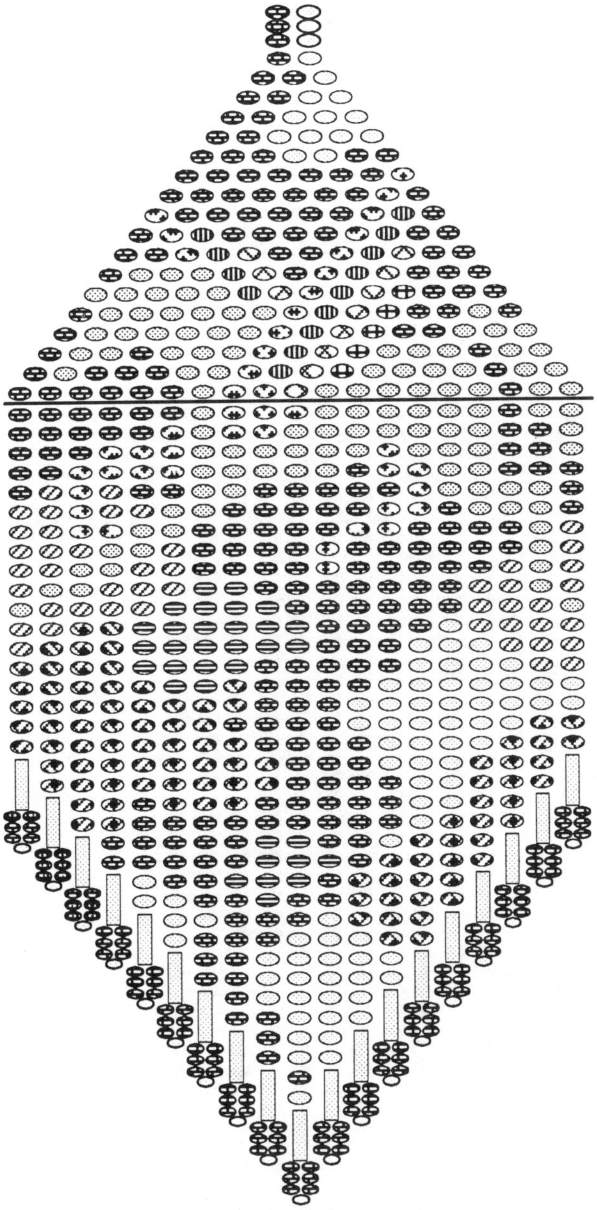

Pattern F: Paint Splatter

Legend

Seed Beads

◔ = 11/o White
◉ = 11/o Orange
◐ = 11/o Dk. Purple
◑ = 11/o Lt. Red
◒ = 11/o Lt. Yellow
● = 11/o Med. Blue

Bugle Beads

▯ = #4 (9mm) White

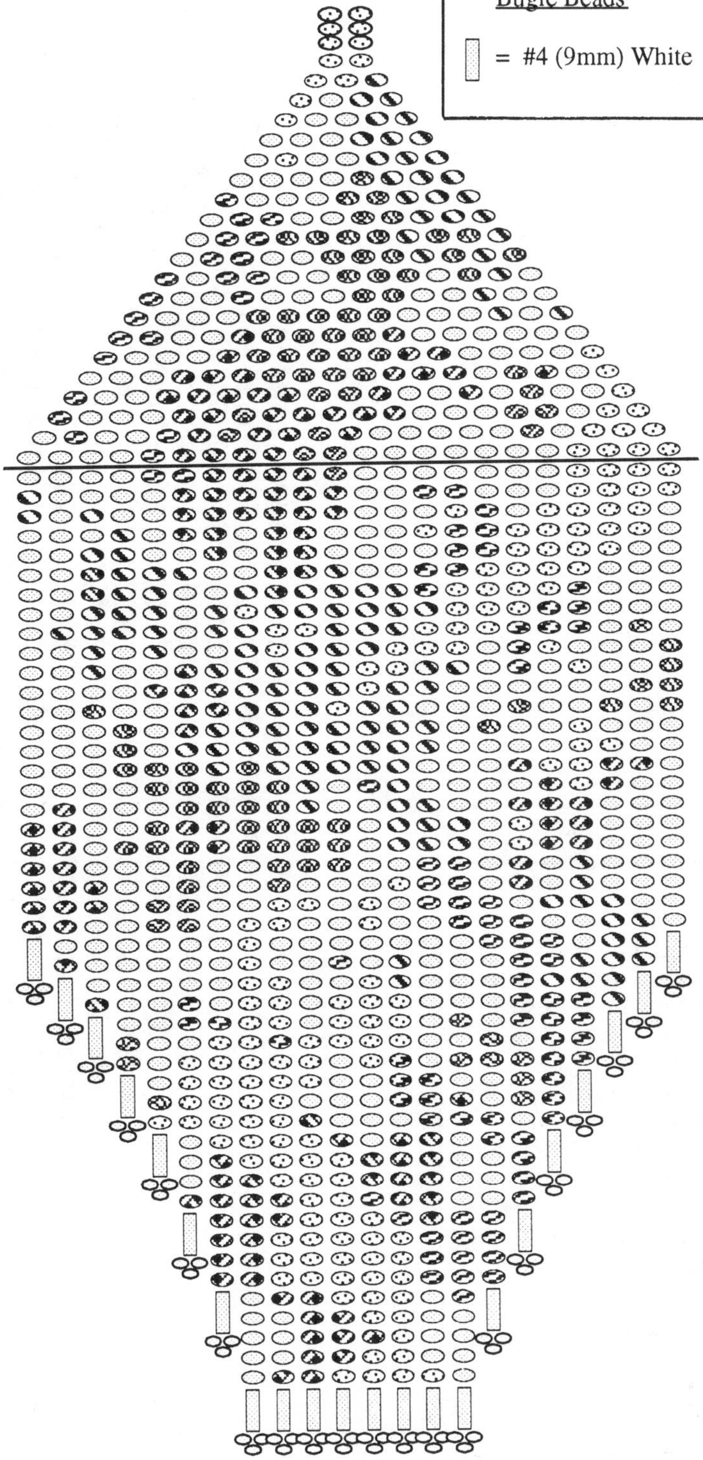

Legend

Seed Beads

⊕ = 11/o Lt. Blue
◉ = 11/o Pearl White
✦ = 11/o Pearl Beige
⊗ = 11/o Pearl Purple
⊕ = 11/o Pearl Peach
⫿ = 11/o Pearl Pink
◯ = 11/o White
⊘ = 11/o Lt. Pink
◐ = 11/o Dk. Purple
⊖ = 11/o Peach

Bugle Beads

▯ = #5 (11mm) White

17

Pattern G: Roses

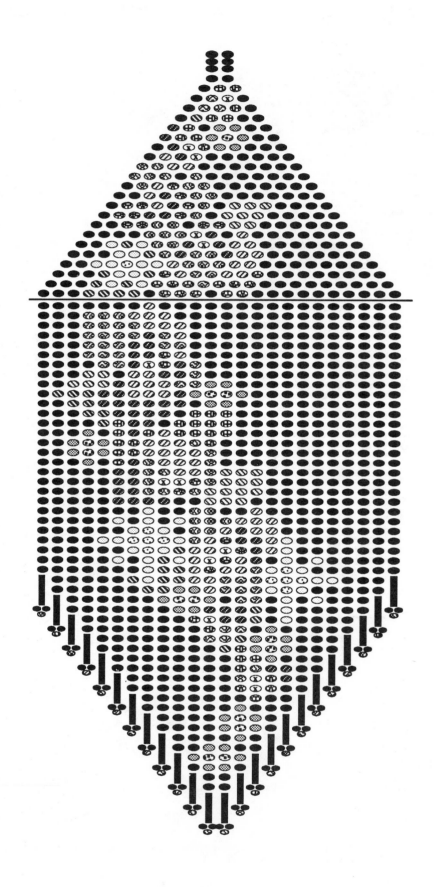

Legend

Seed Beads

- ⬤ = 11/o Black
- 🔘 = 11/o Dk. Green
- 🔘 = 11/o Med. Red
- 🔘 = 11/o Lt. Red
- ⬭ = 11/o White
- 🔘 = 11/o Lt. Yellow
- 🔘 = 11/o Lt. Pink
- ⬤ = 11/o Dk. Red
- 🔘 = 11/o Dk. Pink
- 🔘 = 11/o Lt. Green
- 🔘 = 11/o Pearl White
- 🔘 = 11/o Dk. Yellow

Bugle Beads

- ▮ = 13mm Black

18

Pattern H: Maya

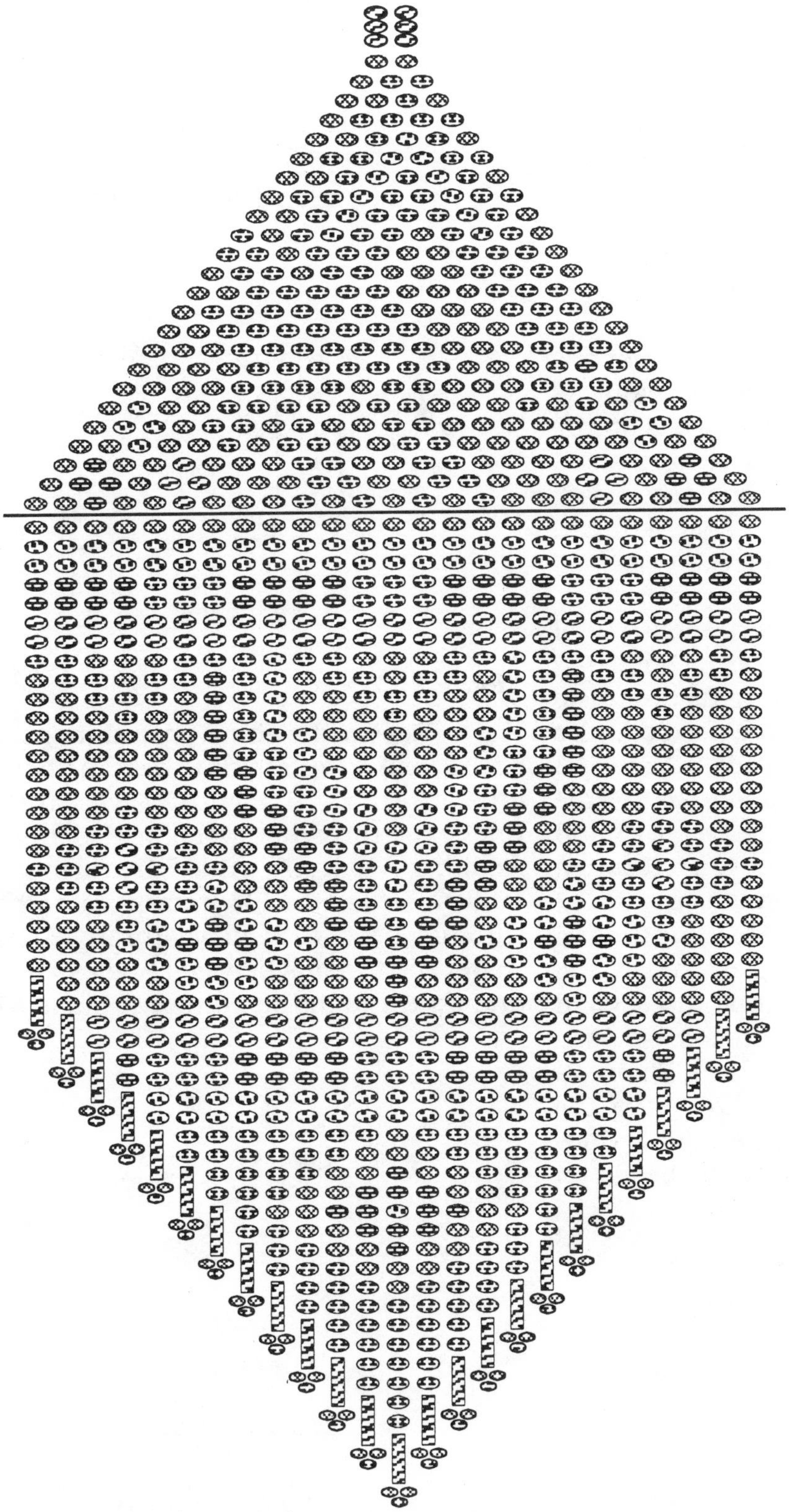

Legend

Seed Beads

⊗ = 11/o Lt. Purple
⊜ = 11/o Lt. Blue
⊘ = 11/o Orange
⊕ = 11/o Aquamarine
⊙ = 11/o Dk. Yellow

Bugle Beads

▨ = #5 (11mm) Orange

Bugle Bead Top - Patterns I to L

Figure 2-26

The top rows of Comanche Stitch earrings can also be made with bugle beads. In addition, seed beads and bugle beads can be combined in a single row, with each set of seed beads equal to the length of one bugle bead. For the purposes of these instructions, a set of seed beads can be treated as if it were a bugle bead.

Four patterns using bugle beads in the top rows of the earring are provided. Suggested materials and colors are provided with each pattern, but feel free to make substitutions. Notice the use of size 2 (3/16") bugle beads in these earrings.

The process of executing the Comanche Stitch with bugle beads is almost the same as with seed beads. The only difference is on the beginning edge of each row, where normally a thread is left showing outside the seed bead. Since bugle beads are so much longer, a thread showing here would be too noticeable, as well as being a potential weak point in construction.

To hide this thread, start each row of bugles (after the base row has been completed using the Ladder Stitch) by stringing two bugle beads onto the thread. Push the needle under the threads between bugle beads #2 and #3 (from back to front). Then push the needle under the threads between bugle beads #1 and #2 (from front to back), and back up through the bottom of the bugle bead on the outside (#7 in Figure 2-25). Pull the thread to bring the two new bugle beads together. Next, push the needle down through the top of the second bugle bead (#8), under the threads between bugles #2 and #3 (from back to front, Figure 2-26), and back up through the bottom of the second bugle bead (#8 in Figure 2-27). Continue stringing the remaining bugle beads on the row as if they were seed beads.

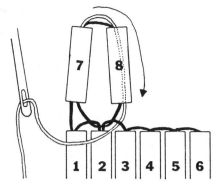

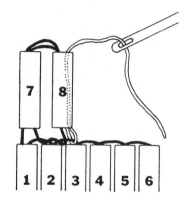

Figure 2-27

Repeat the above procedure at the start of the next row, this time heading back in the other direction. In Figure 2-28 the thread goes under the thread between bugles #9 and #10, from back to front; under the thread between bugles #10 and #11, from front to back; up through bead #12; down through bead #13; under the threads between bugles #9 and #10; and up through the bottom of bugle #13.

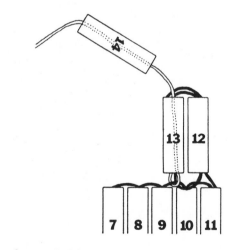

Figure 2-28

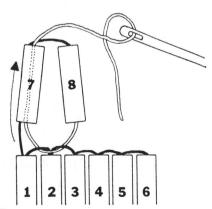

Figure 2-25

20

Pattern I: Rainbow

Legend

Seed Beads
🔵 = 11/o Dk. Blue

Bugle Beads
▨ = #2 (5mm) Dk. Blue
▨ = #2 (5mm) Lt. Purple
▨ = #2 (5mm) Med. Red
▨ = #2 (5mm) Orange
▨ = #2 (5mm) Lt. Yellow
▨ = #2 (5mm) Lt. Green

Pattern J: Mountains

Legend

Seed Beads
⚫ = 11/o Black

Bugle Beads
▨ = #2 (5mm) Silver
▨ = #2 (5mm) Lt. Red
▨ = #2 (5mm) Lt. Purple
■ = #2 (5mm) Black

Pattern K: Tipis

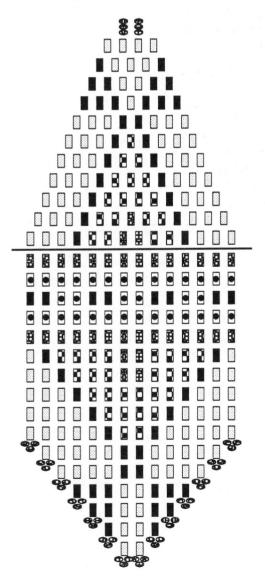

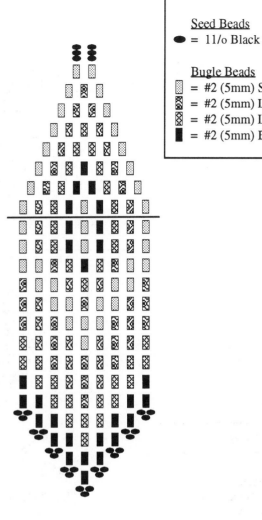

Legend

Seed Beads
🔴 = 11/o Med. Red

Bugle Beads
▯ = #2 (5mm) White
■ = #2 (5mm) Black
▤ = #2 (5mm) Turquoise
▨ = #2 (5mm) Med. Red
◖ = #2 (5mm) Med. Yellow

21

Legend

<u>Seed Beads</u>
⊕ = 11/o Aquamarine
⊛ = 11/o Gold
⊘ = 11/o Dk. Purple
⊕ = 11/o Med. Red

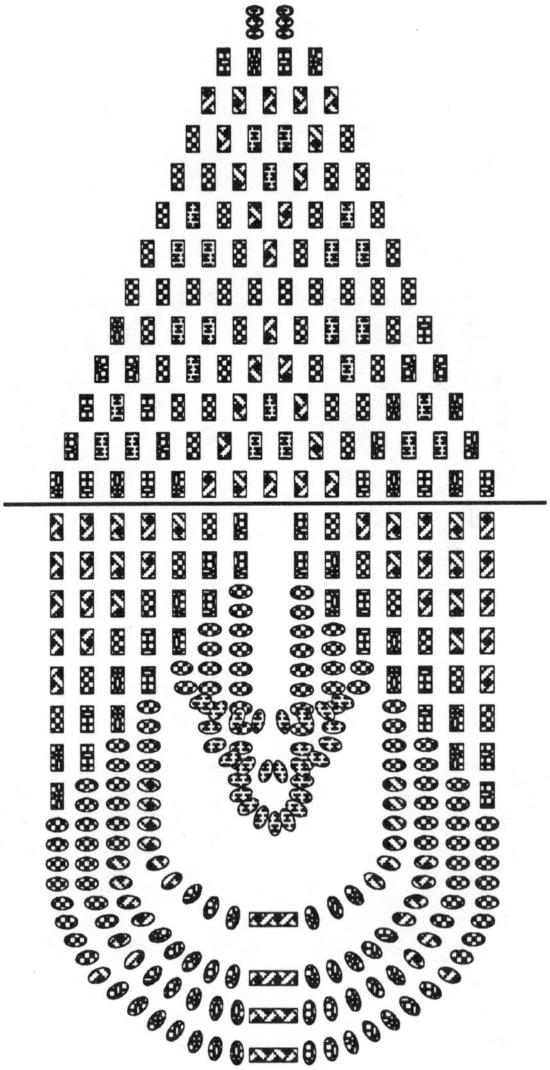

<u>Bugle Beads</u>
▤ = #2 (5mm) Med. Red
▧ = #2 (5mm) Dk. Purple
▤ = #2 (5mm) Aquamarine
▨ = #2 (5mm) Gold

▧ = #5 (11mm) Dk. Purple

Note: inner fringe beads overlap; beads between red bugles are:

5th loop – 2 Green, 8 Aqua, 2 Green
6th loop – 4 Green, 12 Aqua, 4 Green
7th (center) loop – 8 Green, 14 Aqua, 8 Green

NON-LOOM STITCH EARRINGS

Suggested Materials:

> **Sizes 0, A and B Nymo Thread**
> **Size 13 and Size 15 Beading Needles**
> **Size 11/° Seed Beads**
> **Fringe Materials as Desired**
> **Backing Material**
> **Glue**

This stitch imitates the look of beadwork done on a beading loom, but it is produced using a single needle technique called the Non-Loom (or Square) Stitch. The directions for these patterns use the Ladder Stitch and other techniques described and illustrated in the Comanche Stitch chapter; it would be a good idea to read those instructions before beginning a Non-Loom Stitch project.

Odd-Number Earrings - Patterns A to C

Thread a size 13 needle with approximately 3 feet of waxed, size A thread. Stitch the bottom row of Pattern A using seed beads and the Ladder Stitch. When bead #7 has been strung, instead of weaving the thread back through the row (as in the Comanche Stitch), begin the Non-Loom Stitch in row #2 of the pattern.

The aim of the Non-Loom Stitch is to anchor each bead to the ones on either side of it (and to the previous row) with thread. To accomplish this, one bead is strung (Figure 3-1) and anchored by going down through the bead below it (in the previous row), then up through the next bead (forward) in the previous row (Figure 3-2). Then a second bead is strung (Figure 3-3) and anchored by doubling back through the first bead and the one below it. The needle is pushed up through the next bead forward (in the previous row) and back through the second bead strung, ready to add the next bead (Figure 3-4). It is necessary to double back on every other bead strung. Two beads are strung at the beginning of each row and the

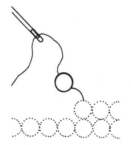

Figure 3-1

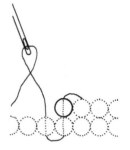

Figure 3-2

Figure 3-3

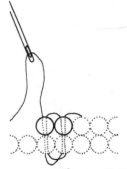

Figure 3-4

second of these is anchored forward as if it were the first bead in the series. This stitch is described in detail for rows #2 and #3.

To start row #2, the needle should be extending upwards out of bead #7 at the right side of the earring (Figure 3-5). String two beads (#8-#9) and anchor bead #9 forward by pushing the needle down through the top of bead #6, then up through the bottom of bead #5 (Figure 3-6).

String a single bead (#10) and double back to anchor it by pushing the needle down

23

through the tops of beads #9 and #6, and then up through the bottoms of beads #5 and #10 (Figure 3-7). String bead #11 and anchor it forward, pushing the needle down through the top of bead #4 and up through the bottom of bead #3 (Figure 3-8).

up through the bottom of bead #12 (Figure 3-10). String bead #17 and double back to anchor it, pushing the needle down through the tops of beads #16 and #13, and up through the bottoms of beads #12 and #17 (Figure 3-11).

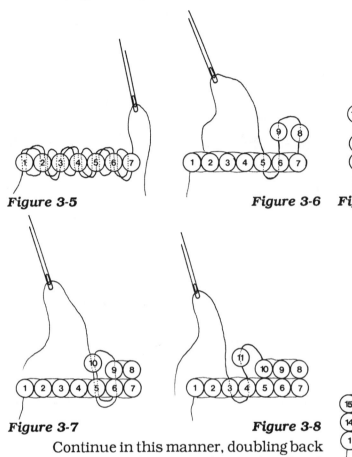

Figure 3-5   **Figure 3-6**

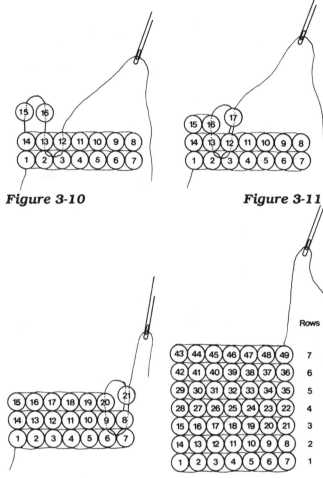

Figure 3-10   **Figure 3-11**

Figure 3-7   **Figure 3-8**

Continue in this manner, doubling back after stringing bead #12, anchoring bead #13 forward, and doubling back after bead #14. This will end row #2 with the needle on the left side of the beadwork, extending upwards out of bead #14 (Figure 3-9).

Figure 3-12   **Figure 3-13**

Continue in this manner, anchoring bead #18 forward, doubling back to anchor bead #19, anchoring bead #20 forward, and doubling back to anchor bead #21. This will end row #3 with the needle extending upwards out of bead #21 on the right side (Figure 3-12).

Continue following Pattern A for bead placement and refer to Figures 3-1 through 3-12 to see how the odd and even-numbered rows should be stitched together. When the last row of this pattern has been completed (Row #7), the needle will be extending out the top of bead #49 on the right side (Figure 3-13).

Insert the needle down through the tops of beads #48, #37, #34, #23, #20, #9, and #6. Then push the needle up and down through the beads of the bottom row, exiting out of bead #2.

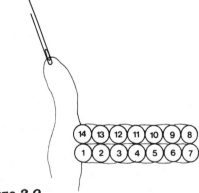

Figure 3-9

To start row #3, string two beads (#15-#16) and anchor bead #16 forward, pushing the needle down through the top of bead #13 and

24

Tie the main thread to the hanging thread with two overhand knots. Hide both threads by weaving them into the body of the earring, then cut them carefully.

Patterns B and C also have an odd number of beads in each row and are done in the same manner as Pattern A. If fringe is desired, attach the segments through the beads in the base row, in the manner described for the Comanche Stitch earrings (see Figure 2-17). Instructions for finishing Non-Loom Stitch earrings are at the end of this chapter (*Attaching the Findings* and *Beaded Borders*).

Pattern A: Bow

Legend
Seed Beads
● = 11/o Gunmetal
⊛ = 11/o Silver

Pattern B: Persian Carpet

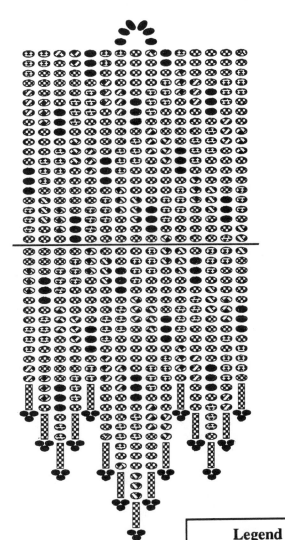

Legend
Seed Beads
⊗ = 11/o Gold
⊘ = 11/o Dk. Purple
⊜ = 11/o Aquamarine
● = 11/o Lt. Red
Bugle Beads
▓ = #5 (11mm) Gold

Pattern C: Op-Art Checks

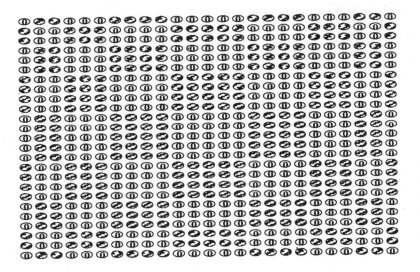

Legend
Seed Beads
⓪ = 13/o Dk. Purple
⊘ = 13/o Orange

Even-Number Earrings - Patterns D to F

Three patterns with an even number of beads in each row are provided. Each legend lists suggested bead colors. The only differences in technique are at the end of odd-numbered rows and, as a result, at the beginning of even-numbered rows. Figure 3-14 shows how to end an odd-numbered row, in this case row #1. The last bead (#8) is ladder-stitched as normal. However, the needle will be coming out of the bottom of bead #8. Start row #2 by putting the needle up through the bottom of bead #7. Then string beads #10 and #9 and anchor them by pushing the needle down through the top of bead #8 and back up through beads #7 and #10 (from the bottom). Continue stitching the rest of the row in the normal

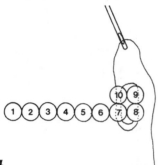

Figure 3-14

Pattern D: Mondrian

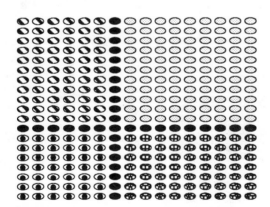

Legend

Seed Beads
◑ = 11/o Med. Yellow
● = 11/o Black
◑ = 11/o Med. Red
◐ = 11/o Med. Blue
○ = 11/o White

Pattern E: Houndstooth

Legend

Seed Beads
○ = 11/o White
● = 11/o Black

Bugle Beads

▯ = #5 (11mm) White

▮ = 25mm Black

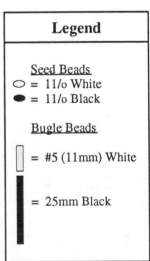

Pattern F: Desert Scene

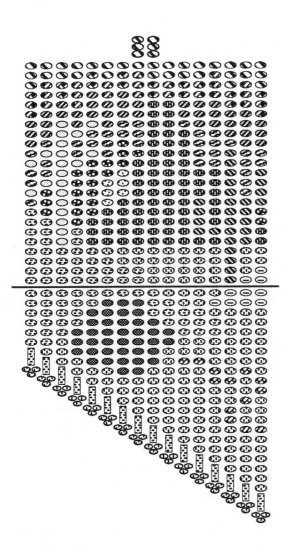

manner.

Bugle Bead Earrings - Patterns G to J

Four patterns are provided which use bugle beads in the Non-Loom Stitch. Each legend lists suggested materials and colors; notice that size 2 (3/16") bugle beads are used in the body of these earrings. The Non-Loom Stitch is executed the same way with bugle beads as it is with seed beads. Because bugle beads are cylinders, the long axis of each bead will be vertical as they are strung together (Figure 3-15).

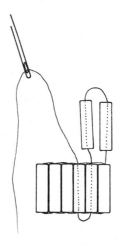

Figure 3-15

Pattern G: Checkerboard

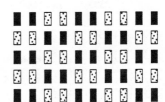

Legend
Seed Beads
☻ = 11/o Dk. Brown
☻ = 11/o Pumpkin
☻ = 11/o Dk. Green
☻ = 11/o Red-Brown
☻ = 11/o White
☻ = 11/o Med. Brown
☻ = 11/o Med. Yellow
☻ = 11/o Orange
☻ = 11/o Lt. Yellow
☻ = 11/o Dk. Pink
☻ = 11/o Lt. Purple
☻ = 11/o Med. Blue
☻ = 11/o Grey
☻ = 11/o Root Beer Brown
Bugle Beads
▤ = #3 (7mm) Dk. Brown

Legend
Bugle Beads
▮ = #2 (5mm) Black
▨ = #2 (5mm) Lt. Yellow

Pattern H: Lightning　　　　　　　　　**Pattern J: Blanket**

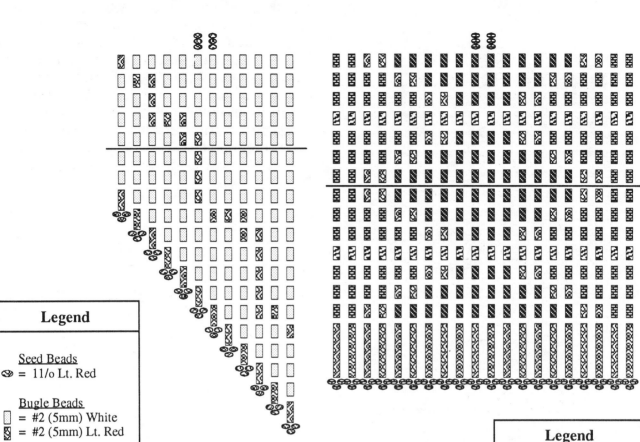

Legend

Seed Beads
⊗ = 11/o Lt. Red

Bugle Beads
▯ = #2 (5mm) White
▨ = #2 (5mm) Lt. Red

▨ = #4 (9mm) Lt. Red

Legend

Seed Beads
⊖ = 11/o Lt. Blue

Bugle Beads
▤ = #2 (5mm) Lt. Blue
▨ = #2 (5mm) Lt. Red
▧ = #2 (5mm) Dk. Blue
▣ = #2 (5mm) Orange

= 15mm Lt. Red

Pattern I: Quilt

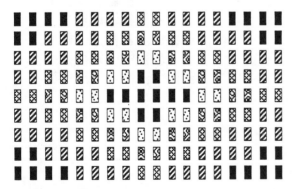

Legend

Bugle Beads
■ = #2 (5mm) Black
▨ = #2 (5mm) Dk. Pink
▨ = #2 (5mm) Lt. Purple
▨ = #2 (5mm) Lt. Red
▨ = #2 (5mm) Lt. Yellow

Attaching the Findings

These earrings can be adapted for any finding. If a style requiring an attachment loop is desired, simply make a loop as shown in the Comanche Stitch instructions. Attach this loop to the two middle beads in the last row of an even-number earring; or in an odd-number earring, attach the loop to the two beads on either side of the single middle bead.

Before attaching a finding with a flat pad, such as a post, a backing material should be sewn onto the beadwork. (The finding can be glued directly to the earring, but the chemicals

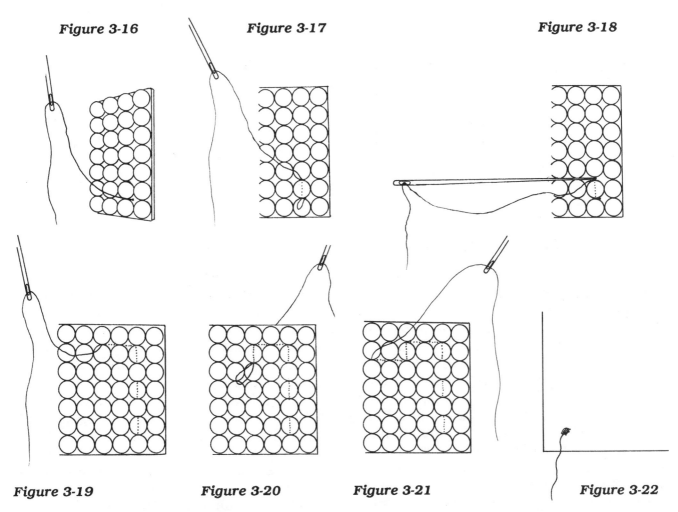

Figure 3-16　　　**Figure 3-17**　　　　　　　**Figure 3-18**

Figure 3-19　　　　**Figure 3-20**　　　**Figure 3-21**　　　**Figure 3-22**

in the glue may alter the color of the beads.)

To add backing material, lay one earring down on the wrong side of a piece of material and trace its shape with a pencil in four places. Cut out the four pieces of backing.

Thread a size 15 needle with size 0 thread and knot one end. Place one of the backing pieces on the earring, with the right side of the material facing the back of the earring. Push the needle through the back of the material, emerging just below the second bead in row #2 of the beadwork (Figure 3-16).

Use a straight running stitch to sew the backing material to the earring. Stitch all the way around the earring, passing through the beads in the second "row" from the outside. To start, pass the needle up through the bottom of the second bead in the second row (Figure 3-17) and then push it through the material, to the back (Figure 3-18). Skip the next bead vertically and bring the needle back up through the material just below the fourth bead in this inside row. Repeat these steps until the next to last bead in this row is reached.

To turn the corner, push the needle

through the next to last bead and then through the material, just above it. Skip the next (third) bead in the new row and bring the needle up through the material just above the fourth bead (Figure 3-19). Push the needle down through the top of this bead (Figure 3-20) and then back.

Skip the next bead and bring the needle up through the material, just below the sixth bead (Figure 3-21). Put the needle up through this bead and back down through the material.

Continue in this manner all the way around the earring. End with the thread on the back of the material. Secure the end of the thread with two or three backstitch knots in the same spot. Leave about 1/4 inch of hanging thread (Figure 3-22).

Position the pad of the earring post on the back of the earring. If the earring is large, position the pad towards the top of the earring (Figure 3-23). On a small earring, such as the one in Pattern A, place the post slightly above center (Figure 3-24). The pad can also be placed so that the earring is worn diagonally (Figure 3-25).

With the pad in position, mark its out-

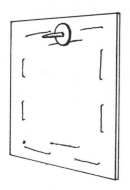

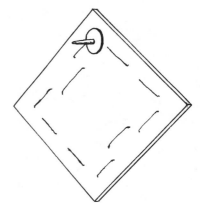

Figure 3-23   *Figure 3-24*   *Figure 3-25*   *Figure 3-26*

line on the backing material with a pen. With the pad still in position, lay the second piece of backing over the finding, making sure it is aligned properly. Take a sewing needle and punch a hole into this piece of backing where the post protrudes. Then push the material over the post to widen the hole (Figure 3-26). If the finding is the clamp or screw type for non-pierced ears, cut a slit large enough to fit the finding through (this slit will be glued back together). Now the earrings are ready to be glued.

Gently squeeze a drop of glue on the marked pad area. Push the pad into position and let this dry for about two hours. After the glue has hardened, use a toothpick to apply a small amount of additional glue to the entire backing area, including the back side of the pad. Make sure the hanging threads from the knots are inside the edges where they will be hidden. Apply glue to the wrong side of the second backing piece, so the right side of the material will face out. Place this backing on the earring, allowing the post to protrude through the hole (Figure 3-27). If a finding for non-pierced ears is used, glue the backing securely over the attachment point and reposition the

slit so that it tightly covers the back of the beadwork. Press the glued sides together tightly and let them dry. Remove any dried glue that has leaked out the sides. At each corner, snip a small triangle off the backing to make the edging application easier (Figure 3-28).

Beaded Borders

A beaded border is a nice way to finish these earrings. Many beaded edging techniques may be used and the choice is based upon the desired appearance of the earring. The beads and colors used in the edging should complement the beads within the earring, and the edging should not overpower the earring design. If no border is applied, the edges of the backing pieces must be sewn together with an overcast stitch, described in the last paragraph of this chapter.

For the earrings in Pattern A, use the following border style, called a Two-Bead Edging or Blanket Stitch. Use one color for the base beads and a contrasting color for the top beads.

Thread a size 15 needle with size B thread and knot one end. Insert the needle between the two backing pieces, above one of the outside rows of beadwork and between the first two beads in this row (Figure 3-29; a & b).

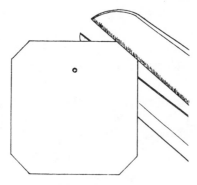

a   *b*

Figure 3-27   *Figure 3-28*   *Figure 3-29*

This hides the knot between the backing pieces.

String a base bead, a top bead and another base bead. Skip the next two beads in the outside row. Push the needle between the third and fourth beads, from front to back, catching the top threads between the beads and passing through both pieces of backing (Figure 3-30). Pull the beads against the earring, and push the needle up through the last

last top bead. Go around the corner and push the needle down through the beginning base bead (Figure 3-34). Then go through both pieces of backing material, from front to back.

Tie the same backstitch knot used when sewing on the backing. Hide the thread end by piercing just the outer backing and emerging between the backing layers, to one side (Figure 3-35). Pull the thread tight and clip it close to

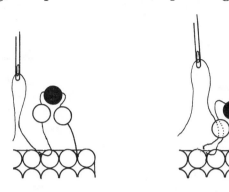

Figure 3-30   **Figure 3-31**

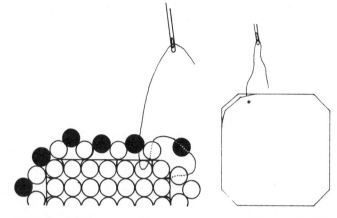

Figure 3-34   **Figure 3-35**

base bead strung (Figure 3-31).

String one top and one base bead. Push the needle through the backing, from front to back, between the fifth and sixth beads in the outer row, and bring the needle up through the last base bead strung (Figure 3-32).

Continue the border in this manner. At each corner, attach a base bead between the next to last bead and the corner bead; this may require skipping only one bead in the outer row. Then string a top bead and a base bead, go around the corner, and attach the base bead just strung between the corner bead and the

the edge of the earring.

Figure 3-36 shows some alternative edging techniques that can be used on any of these earrings. The technique of applying the edging is the same for all of these styles— just remember to choose beads that are found within the earrings, and to choose an edging which does not dominate the earring. One other thing to keep in mind when choosing an edging style: All of these techniques are designed for an even number of beads on each side of the earring. The more beads used in each edging stitch, the more difficult it may be to adjust at the corner

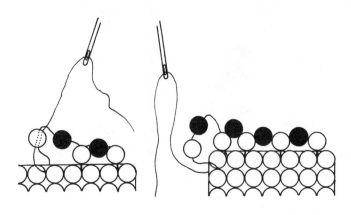

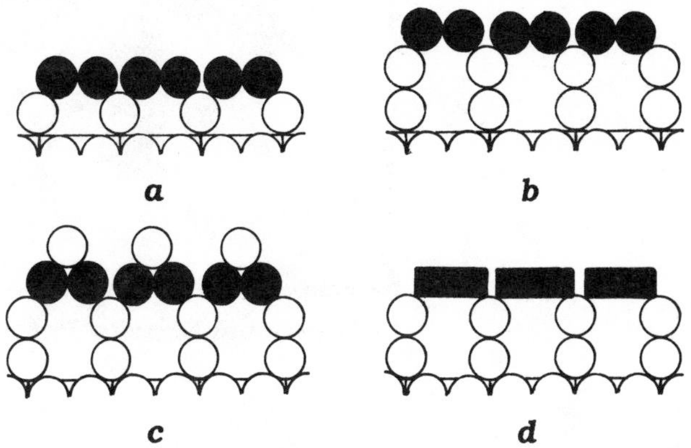

Figure 3-32   **Figure 3-33**

second bead in the new row (Figure 3-33).

To connect the ends of the edging, attach the last base bead at the corner and string the

a   *b*

c   *d*

Figure 3-36

for an odd number of beads.

For earrings with fringe segments, it is not always necessary to apply bead edging behind the fringe (depending upon how much of the earring is visible between fringe segments). Start the edging at the first or second fringe segment and end after one or two segments on the opposite side (Figure 3-37). Continue with an overcast stitch (Figure 3-38) around the earring to the starting point, sewing the edges of the backing together. Stay underneath the fringe on the front of the earring with these stitches. Knot the thread and hide it as before.

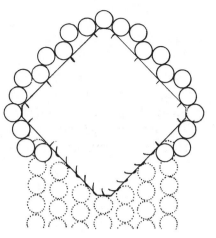

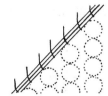

Figure 3-37

Figure 3-38

Non-Loom Stitch: Pattern E (left) & Pattern H (right)

CABOCHON EARRINGS

Suggested Materials:

Size B Nymo Thread
Size 13 and Size 15 Beading Needles
Matching Cabochons
Size 11/° Seed Beads
Fringe Materials as Desired
Backing Material
Glue

Cabochons are available in a wide variety of colors, styles, sizes and shapes. They are jewel-like in appearance and flat on one side. Commonly they are round, square, rectangular or oval in shape and are made of glass, acrylics, minerals or semiprecious stones. Cabochons can be used to make earrings with beads and fringe added, as described in this chapter. Because of the diversity among cabochons, technique is stressed, rather than specific patterns, bead types or colors.

Cabochon Applique Earrings

When choosing cabochons for earrings, select pairs which match each other closely. With glass cabochons, which are usually either plain glass or glass with bits of foil embedded in them, try to find pairs which have matching design elements (i.e., the same colors and foil patterns). Some cabochons have design elements that are at the sides, rather than in the middle. Don't overlook these—just make sure the design elements are in the same area, then rotate the cabochons so that the elements are on opposite sides (mirror images) when the earrings are completed (Figure 4-1).

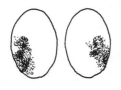

Figure 4-1

Two backing pieces will be needed for each earring. Each piece should be a minimum of 1/4 inch larger than the cabochon in all directions, to allow for the beadwork. The work will be easier if the backing pieces are larger.

Next select the beads and fringe materials (if fringe is desired) for the earrings. Remember to use bead colors that complement the colors and design elements within the cabochons. For example, if the cabochons are blue glass with silver foil elements, try blue and silver beads. Suggestions for fringe patterns are provided in *Getting Started* (see Figure 1-17) and later in this chapter (see Figure 4-12). Lay a string of beads around each cabochon to estimate the number of beads needed (only one row of beads is needed for the main portion of the earring).

Begin by gluing each cabochon to a backing piece, making sure at least 1/4 inch of backing is visible all the way around each one. A clear, flexible glue is an absolute necessity for these earrings. Use a thin, even layer of glue and make sure the backing is flat and smooth, with no wrinkles. Allow the glue to dry at least 24 hours before proceeding.

After the cabochons have dried, again estimate the number of beads needed to fit around each one by wrapping a string of beads around the circumference (Figure 4-2).

Use this number to decide upon a bead pattern; since there is only one row of beads, a repetition pattern is needed. Determine how the circumference number can be divided and what colors will be used in each repetition. For example, if 30 beads fit around a cabochon, five repetitions of a six-bead pattern, such as two silver and four blue beads can be used (Figure 4-3). An example of a five-bead repeatable pattern would be one black, one gold, one blue, one gold and one black bead. If a four-bead pattern is needed, try two red and two white beads.

Figure 4-2   **Figure 4-3**

With the bead pattern decided, thread a size 13 needle with about 1 foot of size B thread and knot one end. Start anywhere on the cabochon and push the needle through the backing material from back to front. Leave enough room for the beads to rest comfortably next to the cabochon without crowding it. A good rule is to leave about half a bead width between the cabochon and the inner edge of the beads (Figure 4-4).

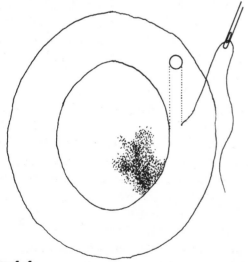

Figure 4-4

The technique used to affix the beads to the backing material is called the Back Stitch. String the first four beads in the pattern, lay them around the cabochon and put the needle

down through the backing at the end of the fourth bead (Figure 4-5). Pull the thread to seat the beads in place— the beads should be snug against each other, but not crowded.

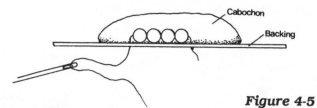

Figure 4-5

Bring the needle up through the backing between the second and third beads (Figure 4-6), and run the needle back through the third and fourth beads (Figure 4-7). String the next four beads, following the pattern decided upon (Figure 4-8).

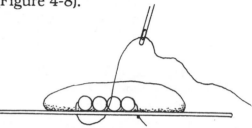

Figure 4-6

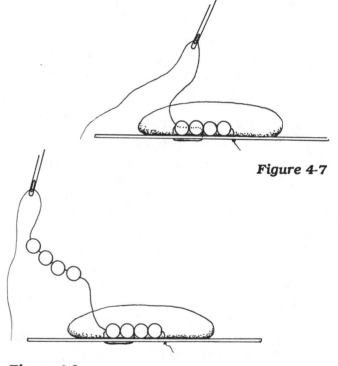

Figure 4-7

Figure 4-8

Lay the new beads around the cabochon and again push the needle down through the backing at the end of the last bead. Remember to keep about half a bead width between the inner edge of the beads and the cabochon as more beads are strung. Bring the needle up through the backing between the sixth and seventh beads strung, and then push it through the seventh and eighth beads.

Repeat the above method of adding new beads until all the beads have been strung. To end the row, bring the needle through the last two beads and then continue through the first two beads strung (Figure 4-9). Put the needle down through the backing material and secure the thread with two or three backstitch knots. Cut the thread, leaving about 1/4 inch of thread hanging from the knots.

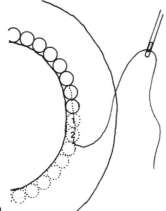

Figure 4-9

With a sharp pair of scissors (not the embroidery scissors used to cut the thread), carefully cut around the perimeter of the beads (do not sever any threads). Leave a small amount (about 1/32 inch) of backing material around the outside of the beads (Figure 4-10).

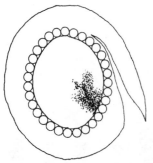

Figure 4-10

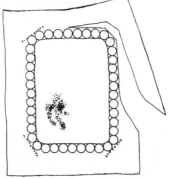

Figure 4-11

If the cabochon is square, snip a small triangle off each corner of the backing, again being careful not to cut any threads (Figure 4-11). Use the beaded cabochons as templates to trace and cut out two more pieces of backing (one for each earring). Put these pieces aside until later.

If fringe is desired, assemble the materials. Suggestions for fringe patterns are provided in Figure 4-12. Line up two or three of the longest segments, side by side, without stringing them. Determine how far apart the fringe segments should be by moving the lined-up segments until the thickest beads in each one are a comfortable distance apart (often a bead width). Then measure the distance between the centers of the top beads in each segment (a in Figure 4-13).

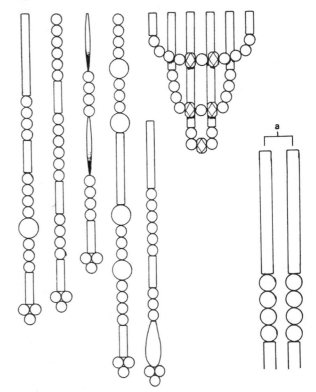

Figure 4-12   **Figure 4-13**

The number of fringe segments which should be used depends upon the size and shape of the cabochon, as well as personal preference. Decide how much of the circumference should be fringed and measure this distance around the cabochon (b in Figure 4-14). Divide the fringed distance (b) by the distance between segments (a) and add 1 to the result. This is the number of fringe segments needed (1 must be added because there will be a fringe segment at the start or zero point of the fringe distance). As an example, if 1 inch of the circumference will be fringed and each fringe segment will be 1/4 inch apart, then the number of segments needed is five. On round or oval cabochons, it is best to use an odd number of fringe segments, with one at the bottom center and an equal number on either side of this center segment.

Find the bottom center of the cabochon and center the area to be fringed around this point. Mark the edges of the fringe area on the backing material of the earring. Two of the fringe segments (or the ends of one loop segment) will be placed on these marks. Divide the fringe area evenly, making marks for each of the remaining fringe segments.

Wax and thread a size 13 needle with a piece of size B thread and knot one end. The length needed is determined by the number and length of fringe segments to be added. Push the needle through the backing, from back to front, on the first fringe mark, about 1/16 inch from the edge (Figure 4-15).

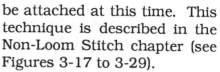

be attached at this time. This technique is described in the Non-Loom Stitch chapter (see Figures 3-17 to 3-29).

Finish the earrings with a beaded border. Use one of the edging styles shown in Figure 4-17 (a to e). The technique for adding an edging is described in the Non-Loom Stitch chapter, along with additional edging styles (see Figures 3-30 to 3-39). Choose beads that incorporate the colors used in the cabochon, and use an edging style that does not overshadow the earring.

Note that the first two edging styles use one base bead and one top bead, with a circumference interval of one bead in style A and two beads in style B.

Edging style C uses a repeating sequence of base beads. Thus the first stitch contains one base bead,

Figure 4-16

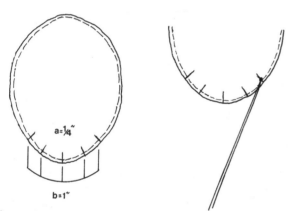

Figure 4-14   *Figure 4-15*

String the desired pattern of fringe materials, including the bottom beads. Push the needle back up through all but the bottom beads and through the backing material, from front to back (Figure 4-16). Pull the thread until the tension is even and correct in this first segment. Then push the needle through the backing on the mark for the second fringe segment and string it, following the same method used for the first fringe segment. Continue in this manner until the last fringe segment has been strung, then secure the thread with two or three backstitch knots in the backing. Be sure to maintain the tension in all the fringe segments as the knots are tied.

If using a finding with a flat pad, it must

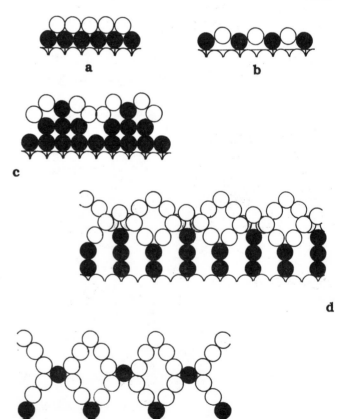

Figure 4-17

one top bead and two base beads. The next stitches have one top bead and three base beads, one top bead and two base beads, and one top bead and one base bead, respectively. In the fifth stitch the sequence begins to repeat with one top and two base beads.

Style D uses two staggered rows of edging, each with a circumference interval of four beads. Add the first row in the regular manner, using sets of two base beads and five top beads. When this row is complete, skip over two circumference beads and add the second edging row in the same manner, using sets of three base beads and five top beads.

Style E adds a second edging row, above (outside) the first row. Complete the first row using sets of two base beads and five top beads. Bring the needle back through the last set of edging beads, emerging from the third (center) top bead. String five beads and run the needle through the next center top bead. Continue in this manner all the way around the cabochon.

If using an earring finding which requires an attachment loop, add this after the edging is completed, but before the thread is knotted. Bring the needle up through the edging base bead(s) on one side of the top center of the earring, string six or eight attachment loop beads, and bring the thread down through the edging base beads on the other side of the center (Figure 4-18).

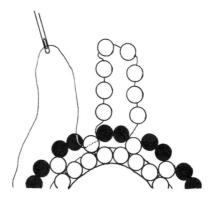

Figure 4-18

To secure the end of the thread, go through both pieces of backing material, from front to back. Tie two or three small backstitch knots. Hide the thread end by piercing just the outer backing and emerging between the backing layers to one side. Pull the thread tight and clip it close to the edge of the earring.

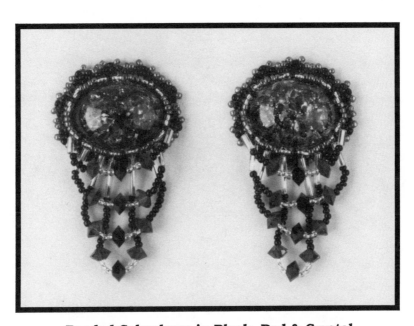

Beaded Cabochons in Black, Red & Crystal

NOTES:

HOW TO BEAD CRYSTALS

Technically, crystals are minerals that take on characteristic geometric shapes and properties, depending upon the environment in which they form. For jewelry uses, the term crystal can also apply to minerals which have been shaped, cut, or even tumbled into polished shapes. Most mineral forms are safe to bead, however, some are too fragile for beadwork; ask questions (or do some research) before buying.

Crystals can be purchased at crystal or rock shops, gem and jewelry shows or flea markets. Local gem and mineral societies can usually suggest a source. Shop carefully because prices vary widely depending on vendor, size, quality and availability.

Some people enjoy crystals for their psychic powers and believe that various minerals possess distinct forces which influence the mind and body. These people insist that the elements used in construction of crystal jewelry be natural. If this is an important consideration, use silk thread and avoid using glue. Some people will accept silicone glue, as silicone is a mineral.

BEADING CYLINDRICAL CRYSTALS

Suggested Materials:

> **Size B Nymo Thread or Silk Thread**
> **Size 15 and Size 16 Beading Needles**
> **Size 13/° Seed Beads *or* Size 12/° 3-Cut Seed Beads**
> **Matching Crystals**
> **Clear Tape or Natural Lining Material**
> **Glue (Optional)**

Two-Drop Peyote Stitch- Patterns A to O

The Peyote Stitch (also known as the Gourd Stitch) was originally used by Native Americans to cover cylindrical objects. It is a particularly good stitch to use on crystals because it grips the objects to which it is applied. This stitch works best on crystals with long shapes, such as quartz or tourmaline (Figure 5-1). For earrings, crystals which are 20 to 40 mm in length work best.

Select two crystals that match each other closely in size, shape and color. These crystals should have edges which are as straight and even in width as possible— extremely tapering sides can cause problems with beading. If one crystal is slightly longer than the other, the difference can be compensated for by starting the beadwork lower; just make sure that the distance from the bottom of the beadwork to the bottom of each crystal is the same.

Determine which will be the top, beaded parts of the crystals and which will be the bottom unbeaded portions. The most attractive, unblemished ends should be the bottoms; in quartz crystals, this is usually the pointed end. Crystals with two good ends can be beaded at either end or in the middle (to hang horizontally).

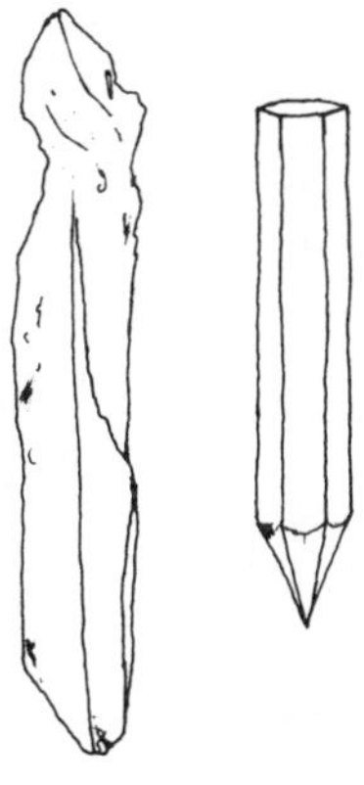

Next decide how much of the crystals will be beaded. These earrings should feature the crystals, so take into account the length of the crystal, and

Figure 5-1

don't overdo the beadwork. Plan on enough beadwork to hold the crystal securely, but not so much that only a small portion of the crystal is visible. Generally at least 3/8 inch of beadwork will be needed; on a long crystal, 3/4 of an inch will still be attractive. The patterns provided for this chapter fall within the 3/8 to 3/4 inch range.

Many crystals have sharp, faceted edges and should be lined to protect the threads in the beadwork from being severed or frayed. Exceptions are crystals formed from soft minerals, such as fluorite octahedrons, or smooth-sided crystals, such as tourmaline, aquamarine, or any mineral polished into a tubular form. The lining is also used to make the circumferences of both crystals the same and to smooth the surfaces for beading. If concerned about natural materials, use thin leather, cotton or wool material; if not, use clear tape.

Cut pieces of lining to fill in depressions or correct tapering edges (Figure 5-2). Tape can be applied as each piece is cut; material pieces can be glued, or they can be held in place by the the final layer, which is sewn. If one crystal is thinner than the other, wrap additional lining material around it until the circumferences of the two crystals are the same. Always end with one even layer over the entire beading area to provide a smooth beading surface (Figure 5-3). If material is used, attach this final layer with a needle and thread. Hide the knot on the inside of the lining material and sew the edges together tightly with a whip stitch (Figure 5-4). If tape is used, extend the lining about 1/4 inch below the intended beading area.

area must be measured. First, take a string of beads and wrap it around each crystal at the bottom of the area to be beaded. Determine how many beads it takes to fit around each one (Figure 5-5); this should be the same number for both crystals. The Two-Drop Peyote Stitch requires an even number of circumference beads. If the beads do not total an even number, decrease the number by one (e.g., if the circumference measures 33 beads, make the bead total 32).

Next measure the approximate height of the beadwork area by aligning beads, side by side, along the length of the lined area (Figure 5-6). Since strung beads can not be used for this measurement (as the beads will not be aligned in this manner when stitched around the crystal), it is helpful to construct a bead ruler or gauge. To do this, sew a line of seed beads together with the Ladder Stitch (see Figures 2-1 to 2-6). If possible, use two beads each of several different colors to help in counting the number of beads. This Ladder Stitch gauge can be used for many other projects.

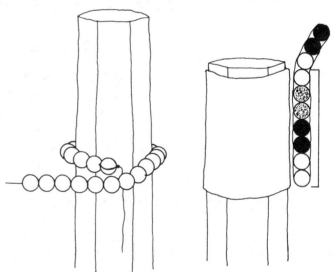

Figure 5-5   **Figure 5-6**

Use these measurements as an aid and choose one of the Peyote Stitch patterns. Peyote Stitch patterns are repetitive, thus they can be multiplied to fit around the circumference of a crystal. Each pattern lists the minimum number of circumference beads, the number of beads which must be added to repeat the pattern horizontally (around the crystal) and the bead height of the pattern vertically (as measured by a bead gauge). Be aware that the bead gauge measurement is approximate; the actual height of the beadwork will depend on

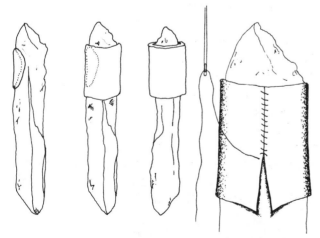

Figure 5-2   Figure 5-3   Figure 5-4

Before selecting a Peyote Stitch pattern, the circumference and height of the beading the tightness of the stitching and the uniformity of the beads.

Use the less complicated, shorter patterns on small crystals and save the more complex patterns for large crystals. On large crystals, it is possible to repeat a short pattern vertically, or to use a short pattern and fill the excess beading area by using a single color above and below the pattern. When planning deviations such as this, remember that each row of Peyote Stitch adds about half a bead width in height.

As an example, Pattern E (Stripes) is a design which uses multiples of two in the circumference; three repetitions of the pattern are shown. For a crystal with 12 beads in the circumference, use six repetitions of the two-bead design; for a crystal with 20 beads in the circumference, use 10 repetitions of the two-bead design. This pattern repeats vertically after eight rows of beading and is about five bead widths high due to the staggered nature of the rows in this stitch.

Figure 5-7 shows how the bead numbers used in the directions for the Peyote Stitch fit into a pattern. Remember that the beadwork is done from bottom to top, so it is essential to follow the pattern from the bottom up. Colors are suggested for each pattern, but the actual colors used should complement the color(s) of the crystal. If a clear crystal is used, then the suggested colors are appropriate.

After preparing the crystals and selecting a pattern, thread a size 15 needle with 1-1/2 to 3 feet of waxed thread. The amount of thread depends upon the size of the crystal and how much beadwork will be applied.

If the crystal is lined with material, knot one end of the thread and anchor the first row by piercing the lining material at the bottom, from the inside out, to hide the knot (Figure 5-

8). String half of the total number of circumference beads, lay them around the crystal and run the needle through the first bead (#1a) strung (Figure 5-9). Pull the thread tight.

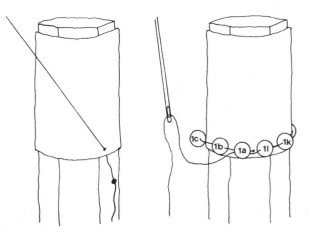

Figure 5-8   **Figure 5-9**

If the crystal is lined with clear tape, string half of the number of circumference beads on the thread. Wrap the beads around the crystal near the bottom of the tape lining (below the intended beadwork area) and tie a square knot. Leave a hanging thread. Tighten the tension and tie an overhand knot to prevent the square knot from slipping. Run the needle through the first bead (#1a) strung and pull the thread tight.

In either case, space this first row of beads evenly around the crystal to allow the beads in the next row to nest between them. Remember the number of beads strung for the first row— the same number will be added to each row, and remembering it will lessen confusion at the start of each new row.

String the first bead of the second row (#2a). Push the needle down through the second bead (#1b) of the first row (Figure 5-10) and tighten the thread so that bead #2a sits above and between beads #1a and #1b. String

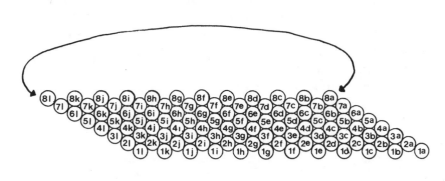

Figure 5-7

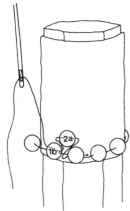

Figure 5-10

the next bead (#2b) of the second row. Continue to alternately push the needle down through the first row beads and add second row beads. Maintain a tight tension throughout this stitch, as this allows the beads to firmly hold the crystal.

If the crystal is lined with material, tack the beadwork to the lining at equal distances around the crystal as the second row is added. Do this by taking a stitch in the lining material, behind one of the beads in the first row, before adding the next bead in the second row (Figure 5-11).

When the same number of beads has been strung in the second row as in the first, finish the row by pushing the needle through bead #1a and then up through bead #2a (Figure 5-12). This positions the thread to begin adding the third row.

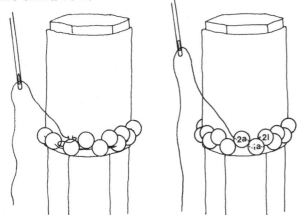

Figure 5-11   **Figure 5-12**

Notice that the beads in the second row are raised slightly above those in the first row (Figure 5-13). The beads for each new row are strung between the raised beads of the previous row and, when complete, the new row will be slightly raised in the same manner. This gives the Peyote Stitch a spiral appearance, because each new row lays slightly to the left of the previous row (Figure 5-14). It is very easy to become confused about which row is being worked on, and where the next row should start. By counting the spiral beads as illustrated and remembering to count each bead as it is strung, it should be easy to keep track of where to end each row.

The third row of beads will start to anchor the beadwork to the crystal. As each bead is applied in this row, press it up towards the crystal to bind the beadwork tightly (Figure 5-15). When the last bead of the row has been

strung, push the needle through the first bead (#2a) of the second row and then through the first bead (#3a) of the third row (see Figure 5-12). Continue adding rows of beads using the same technique and following the chosen pattern for bead color and placement.

Remember to finish each row by stringing the last bead, going through the first bead of the previous row, and then through the first bead of the row being completed (see Figure 5-12). If the crystal is lined with material, secure every third row or so to the lining (see Figure 5-11).

When the last row is finished, push the needle clockwise through all the beads in this top row, ending with the last bead added (Figure 5-16).

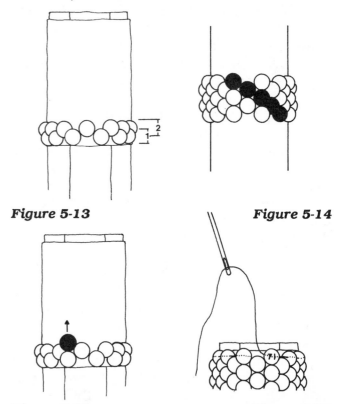

Figure 5-13   **Figure 5-14**

Figure 5-15   **Figure 5-16**

Now decide which sides of each crystal should be the front and back of the earring. The front side should have the least number of flaws in both the crystal and the beadwork. Once this is decided, push the needle around through the top row of beads until it is through the "middle" bead, between the front and back halves of the earring on one side. This is an attachment loop anchor bead.

Decide how many beads are needed to make the attachment loop, allowing for a space of 1/8 to 1/4 inch above the top of the longest crystal. There must be an even number of loop beads and the same number should be used on both earrings (Figure 5-17).

String the proper number of loop beads, using a pattern and color combination that complements the beads used on the crystal. Locate the second loop anchor bead on the opposite side of the crystal. If there are an even number of top row beads, there will be the same number of beads on either side of the loop anchor beads (Figure 5-18). With an odd number of top row beads, put one more bead on the front side than is between the anchor beads on the back side. Enter the second anchor bead from the same side of the bead (front or back) that the thread left the first anchor bead and pull the thread through.

If the crystal was lined with tape, put the needle on the hanging thread at the bottom of the beadwork. Go counterclockwise up the nearest bead towards the back of the earring and up the spiral row to exit out the center of the work.

Remember that on crystals lined with tape, the beadwork was started below the intended beadwork area. This is so it can be pushed up and glued in place. Place a small amount of glue on the tape lining near the top of the beadwork, on the back side of the earring (Figure 5-22). Gently push the beadwork up into place. Cut both threads flush with the beadwork and apply glue to these areas, as well as to both of the knots.

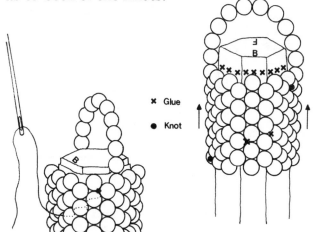

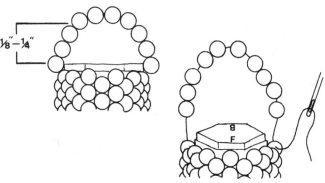

Figure 5-17   **Figure 5-18**

Go back through the loop beads and the first anchor bead, entering the anchor bead from the other side (Figure 5-19). Adjust the tension in the attachment loop, then go down through the closest bead towards the back of the earring and tie two overhand knots (Figure 5-20). Do <u>not</u> cut the thread. Continue clockwise down the spiral row to the middle of the beaded area and then exit the beadwork (Figure 5-21). If the crystal was lined with material, cut the main thread flush with the beadwork.

Figure 5-21   **Figure 5-22**

Once the glue has dried, take a craft knife and carefully cut the excess tape from the bottom of the crystal. To avoid cutting any threads, tilt the blade away from the beads. Remove the excess tape and trim off any that is visible around the bottom edge.

Pattern A: Zig-Zag 1

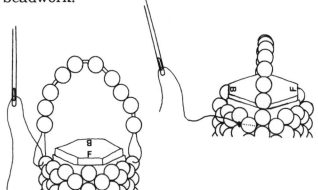

Figure 5-19   **Figure 5-20**

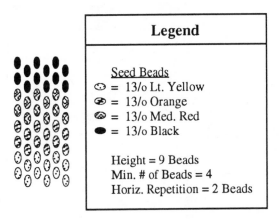

Legend
Seed Beads
😊 = 13/o Lt. Yellow
😊 = 13/o Orange
😊 = 13/o Med. Red
● = 13/o Black
Height = 9 Beads
Min. # of Beads = 4
Horiz. Repetition = 2 Beads

Pattern B: Zig-Zag 2

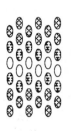

Legend
Seed Beads ⊗ = 13/o Lt. Purple ⊕ = 13/o Aquamarine ◯ = 13/o Clear Height = 7 Beads Min. # of Beads = 4 Horiz. Repetition = 2 Beads

Pattern C: Zig-Zag 3

Legend
Seed Beads ⊗ = 13/o Silver ◯ = 13/o Clear ⊗ = 13/o Dk. Purple Height = 5 Beads Min. # of Beads = 4 Horiz. Repetition = 2 Beads

Pattern D: Stripes 1

Legend
Seed Beads ⊗ = 13/o Lt. Blue ⊗ = 13/o Powder Blue ⊗ = 13/o Med. Blue ⊗ = 13/o Dk. Blue Height = 4 Beads Min. # of Beads = 4 Horiz. Repetition = 2 Beads

Pattern E: Stripes 2

Legend
Seed Beads ⊗ = 13/o Pink ⬤ = 13/o Black Height = 5 Beads Min. # of Beads = 4 Horiz. Repetition = 2 Beads

Pattern F: Stripes Plus 1

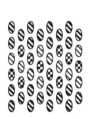

Legend
Seed Beads ⊗ = 13/o Dk. Green ⊗ = 13/o Lt. Green ⊗ = 13/o Gold Height = 6 Beads Min. # of Beads = 8 Horiz. Repetition = 4 Beads (Note: 1/2 # of beads to start <u>must</u> be an even #.)

Pattern G: Stripes Plus 2

Legend
Seed Beads ⬤ = 13/o Black ⊗ = 13/o Gold ⊗ = 13/o Silver Height = 6 Beads Min. # of Beads = 8 Horiz. Repetition = 4 Beads

Pattern H: Triangles & Diamonds 1

Legend
Seed Beads ⬤ = 13/o Black ⊘ = 13/o Orange ⊗ = 13/o Pink ⊗ = 13/o Lt. Red Height = 6 Beads Min. # of Beads = 8 Horiz. Repetition = 4 Beads

Pattern I: Triangles & Diamonds 2

Legend
Seed Beads ⬤ = 13/o Black ⊗ = 13/o Gold Height = 5 Beads Min. # of Beads = 8 Horiz. Repetition = 4 Beads

Pattern J: Triangles & Diamonds 3

Legend

Seed Beads
- ⊕ = 13/o Med. Red
- ⊗ = 13/o Dk. Blue
- ○ = 13/o White

Height = 8 Beads
Min. # of Beads = 8
Horiz. Repetition = 4 Beads

Pattern K: Triangles & Diamonds 4

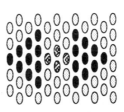

Legend

Seed Beads
- ○ = 13/o White
- ● = 13/o Black
- ⊗ = 13/o Lt. Red

Height = 6 Beads
Min. # of Beads = 24
Horiz. Repetition = 12 Beads
(Note: only one repetition
shown here.)

Pattern L: Triangles & Diamonds 5

Legend

Seed Beads
- ⊘ = 13/o Dk. Purple
- ⊗ = 13/o Gold
- ⊛ = 13/o Silver
- ⊖ = 13/o Lt. Blue
- ⊕ = 13/o Med. Red

Height = 7 Beads
Min. # of Beads = 12
Horiz. Repetition = 6 Beads
(Note: only one repetition
shown here.)

Pattern M: Triangles & Diamonds 6

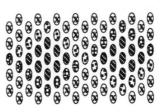

Legend

Seed Beads
- ⊗ = 13/o Lt. Blue
- ⊛ = 13/o Dk. Yellow
- ● = 13/o Dk. Blue
- ⊕ = 13/o Med. Red

Height = 6 Beads
Min. # of Beads = 38
Horiz. Repetition = 16 Beads
(Note: only one repetition
shown here.)

Pattern N: Flowers 1

Legend

Seed Beads
- ⊗ = 13/o Lt. Purple
- ⊘ = 13/o Lt. Pink
- ⊖ = 13/o Turquoise
- ⊗ = 13/o Orange
- ⊙ = 13/o Med. Yellow

Height = 8 Beads
Min. # of Beads = 8
Horiz. Repetition = 4 Beads

Pattern O: Flowers 2

Legend

Seed Beads
- ● = 13/o Dk. Blue
- ⊕ = 13/o Lt. Blue
- ⊗ = 13/o Dk. Green
- ⊙ = 13/o Lt. Yellow
- ⊙ = 13/o Orange
- ⊛ = 13/o Lt. Red

Height = 10 Beads
Min. # of Beads = 8
Horiz. Repetition = 4 Beads

BEADING SPHERICAL CRYSTALS

Suggested Materials:

> Size B Nymo Thread or Silk Thread
> Size 15 and Size 16 Beading Needles
> Size 13/° Seed Beads *or* Size 12/° 3-Cut Seed Beads
> Matching Crystals

Netted Covering

A netted covering is an attractive and simple way to bead around spherical or marble-shaped crystals. Findings can be attached to the beadwork without touching the crystal. The net consists of six beaded triangles, attached to a central ring of beads. Three of the triangles are pulled together at the top of the crystal and three at the bottom, creating a bag or net of beads to hold the crystal.

To begin, measure the circumference of the crystal at its thickest point with a string of beads (Figure 6-1). If the number of beads measured is not divisible by six, add extra beads so that it is (i.e., 12, 18, 24, etc.). Thread a size 15 needle with about 2 feet of waxed thread and string this number of beads in one color. Before putting the beads around the crystal, tie them in a tight circle with a square knot. Leaving a hanging thread of about six inches, push the needle clockwise through the first two beads (Figure 6-2). The thread is now coming out of the first anchor bead for the triangles.

Place the circle of beads around the crystal and measure with a string of beads from the circle to the top (and/or bottom) of the crystal in two or three places (Figure 6-3). Be aware that this method of measuring the length of the netting segments is approximate. Due to irregularities in the crystal and differences in individual beads, it may be necessary to redo the triangles before the crystal can be put in the netting. In a different color, string the largest number of beads measured plus one extra. (In Figure 6-3, five beads were measured, so six beads should be strung.)

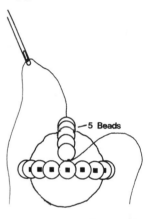

Figure 6-3

Add one bead of the first color and then push the needle down through the next to last bead strung (Figure 6-4). To complete the first triangle, string the original number of beads measured (five in the example; Figure 6-5).

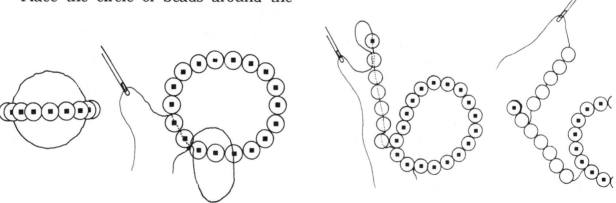

Figure 6-1   *Figure 6-2*   *Figure 6-4*   *Figure 6-5*

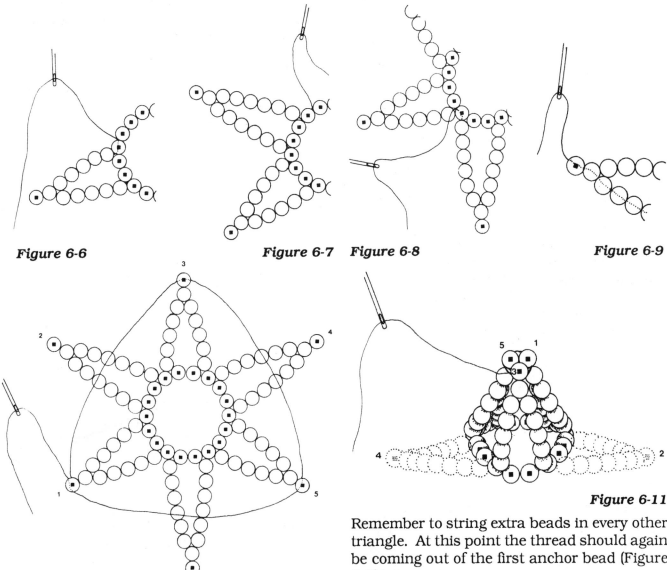

Figure 6-6   Figure 6-7   Figure 6-8   Figure 6-9

Figure 6-10

Figure 6-11

Remember to string extra beads in every other triangle. At this point the thread should again be coming out of the first anchor bead (Figure 6-8).

Push the needle up through the closest arm of the first triangle and through the single bead on the top (Figure 6-9). Make sure the thread through the top bead is not twisted. Push the needle through the top beads of triangles #3 and #5, and through the top bead of triangle #1 again (Figure 6-10). Pull the thread tight, bringing the tops of the three triangles together. Run the needle through all three top beads again, then through the top bead of triangle #3 (Figure 6-11).

Bring the needle down through the arm of triangle #3 which is closest to triangle #4 (Figure 6-12) and go through the anchor bead at the bottom of this arm. Now thread the needle through the arm of triangle #4 which is attached to this same anchor bead. Continue up through the bead at the top of this triangle (Figure 6-13).

To determine how many beads to skip between anchor beads, subtract 6 from the total number of circumference beads, and divide the result by 6. (For example, if there are 18 circumference beads, subtract 6 and divide the result [12] by 6. The answer is 2.) Skip this number of circumference beads and push the needle clockwise through the next anchor bead (Figure 6-6). Pull the thread tight and push the beads in the triangular segment toward the circumference beads until all the beads are snug against one another.

For the second triangle, add one extra bead to each side of the triangle (Figure 6-7). Don't forget the single first color bead at the top of the triangle. Repeat the process of stringing triangle segments (as illustrated in Figures 6-4 to 6-7) until six triangles have been strung.

47

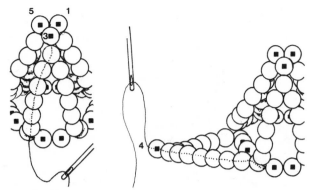

Figure 6-12   Figure 6-13

Flip the netting so that the joined tri-angles (#1, #3 and #5) are at the bottom. Run the needle through the three remaining top beads (triangles #6, #2 and #4), but do not pull them together (Figure 6-14). Insert the crystal into the netting and pull the thread tight (Figure 6-15). Go through all three top beads again.

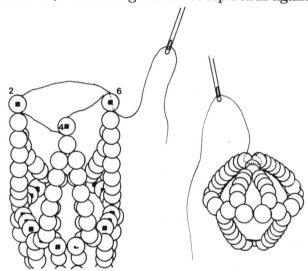

Figure 6-14   Figure 6-15

Make an attachment loop by stringing six beads; two of the second color, two of the first color and two of the second color. Insert the needle into the far side of top bead #2 and continue back through the attachment loop beads (Figure 6-16). Push the needle through top bead #6 (from the side closest to bead #2) and then back through the attachment loop.

Push the needle through top bead #2, down through one of the arms of triangle #2 and into the nearest anchor bead. Continue around the circumference and exit by the hanging thread. Knot the two threads together, hide the ends within the triangle arms and clip any excess thread.

Pebble-shaped crystals can also be

beaded with a netted cover. Put the circumference row at the mid point of the crystal and add an extra bead or two to the triangular segments to account for any irregularities in shape (Figure 6-17). Crystals that are long and irregular should be beaded with the Peyote Stitch, using the lining material to even out any differences in circumference size.

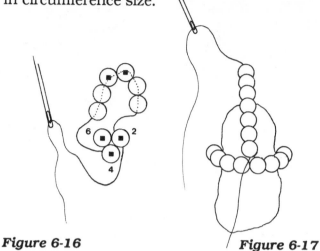

Figure 6-16   Figure 6-17

Modified Comanche Stitch

Spherical crystals can also be beaded with a modified version of the Comanche Stitch. In this version, beads are added above and below a central circumference row. The number of beads in each row decreases, and the amount of decrease depends upon the size of the crystal and the size of the beads. Because of these discrepancies, the instructions given are rather general. The only patterns recommended are horizontal stripes, which can be achieved by changing colors at the start of a new row. Nymo thread is preferable for this stitch, because it stretches and provides the flexibility required for this technique. Also, read the Comanche Stitch instructions (see Figures 2-8 to 2-14) if this procedure is not already familiar.

Use a Ladder Stitch gauge (see Figure 5-7) to determine the number of beads to string around the center of the crystal, or just start sewing beads together with the Ladder Stitch and periodically measure around the crystal to see if enough beads have been added. Use a size 15 needle and about 3 feet of thread. Sew enough beads together to fit tightly around the circumference of the crystal, then connect the ends by threading the needle through the first bead strung and back through the last bead strung (Figure 6-18). Be careful not to twist the string of beads and keep the hanging thread on the left.

In the illustrated example, row #1 has 17 beads, #1a through #1q. Use the Comanche Stitch technique on the second row of beads, but start the row by adding two beads (#2a & #2b), as is done when stringing bugle beads. Push the needle under the top threads between beads #1p & #1o, from the inside of the circle out. Go under the top threads between beads #1q & #1p, from the outside in, and up through bead #2a (Figure 6-19). Go down through bead #2b, under the thread between beads #1p and #1o again, and back up through bead #2b (Figure 6-20).

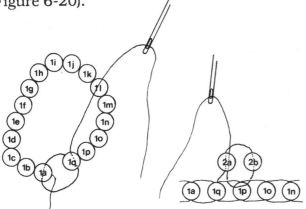

Figure 6-18   *Figure 6-19*

To decrease the circumference of the beadwork enough to fit around the crystal, several beads must be skipped in the second row. Do this on the next bead. String on bead #2c and go under the threads between beads #1o and #1n— from the inside out, as is normal. Instead of simply going back up through bead #2c, however, go between beads #1n and #1m— from the outside in— and then back up through bead #2c, thus skipping a bead (Figure 6-21). Add bead #2d in the normal manner, going under the threads between beads #1m and #1l, and straight back up through bead #2d.

The size of the crystal determines how many beads must be skipped in the second row, so the following instructions are approximate. Do <u>not</u> put the crystal into the beadwork at this point. Instead, use the Ladder Stitch gauge to measure the crystal and get a feel for the number of beads required in the second row. Start by skipping a bead as every third bead is added (i.e., use the stitch to skip a bead when adding beads #2c, #2f, #2i, etc.) and see if the new row is developing the right circumference. On large spheres (e.g., 20 mm in diameter), a bead may only need to be skipped after every four or five beads added normally. Even on small spheres (e.g., 13mm), however, if a bead is skipped with each stitch the second row will be too narrow to fit the crystal. Estimating how many beads to skip becomes easier with experience.

To end the second row, run the needle down through bead #2a and back up through the last bead added (see Figure 6-18).

Start the third row in the same way as the second. If the sphere is small, this will be the final row on this half of the beading and no beads should be skipped. If the sphere is large, beads may have to be skipped after every fifth or sixth bead added normally and one or two more rows added. Keep in mind that this is only the top half of the beadwork— limit the number of rows so that the top one-third of the crystal will remain unbeaded. Make sure the last row is strung with no beads skipped.

End the final row on this side of the center row in the same manner as the previous rows (see Figure 6-18). Then push the needle down through the first bead of the final row and continue down through the closest beads in the rows below it. Exit out the bottom of the first (center) row (Figure 6-22).

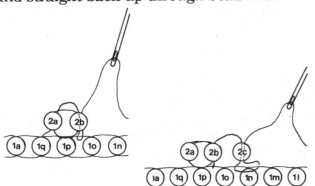

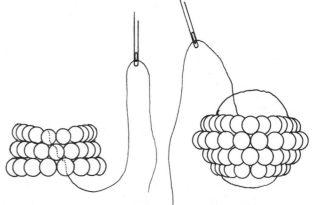

Figure 6-20   *Figure 6-21*   *Figure 6-22*   *Figure 6-23*

Flip the beadwork over so that the needle is at the top, with the beadwork below it. Add a row of beads on the other side of the center row (now at the top) in the same manner as the original second row.

When this row is completed, put the beadwork on the crystal and position it so that the center row is at the widest part of the sphere (Figure 6-23). If there are interesting features of the crystal, such as striations of color, position them so that they can be seen above and below the beadwork. Any flaws in the crystal, such as cracks or dark inclusions, should be hidden beneath the beadwork.

At this point it will be difficult to keep the beadwork on the crystal, because it will be a tight fit as the threads stretch to accommodate the sphere. It is generally easier to hold the crystal portion while beading to keep the stress on the beadwork to a minimum.

Add the same number of rows to this half of the beadwork as were added to the first half. String the last row without skipping any beads and then thread the needle down through the completed rows. Exit at the bottom of row #2, just above the center row (Figure 6-24). This is the first anchor bead for the attachment loop.

String six loop beads, skip the center row, and anchor the loop in the next row, directly below the first anchor bead (Figure 6-25). Be sure to enter the second anchor bead from the center row side. Thread the needle back through the attachment loop beads. Go through the first anchor bead again, this time from the side above the second row.

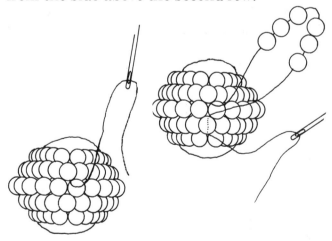

Figure 6-24   *Figure 6-25*

Switch to a size 16 needle and weave the thread horizontally through the beadwork to the hanging thread (Figure 6-26), knot the two threads and weave the ends into the beadwork to hide them. Clip off any excess thread.

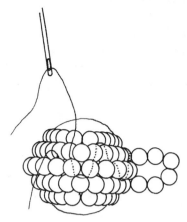

Figure 6-26

Three-Drop Peyote Stitch

Round crystals can also be beaded with the Peyote Stitch, but a Three-Drop variation is used. This variation has the advantage of holding whatever it covers more tightly, and it also adapts to changes in shape more readily. The beading is done on a tapered object of the same circumference as the crystal, such as a tapered felt-tip pen. The Three-Drop Peyote Stitch can also be used on cylindrical objects.

Although patterns can be devised for the Three-Drop Peyote Stitch (similar to those for the Two-Drop Peyote Stitch), differences in sphere size make it simpler to use zig-zag designs on round crystals. Zig-zags are created by using one color for rows #1 and #2, a second color for rows #3 and #4, and a third color for rows #5 and #6.

Begin by measuring the circumference of the sphere at its widest point with a string of beads. The key to this stitch is that the total number of beads used for the circumference must be divisible by 3, and when one-third of the circumference beads are removed, there must be an even number of beads remaining. For example, 42 beads in total circumference divided by 3 equals 14; 14 subtracted from 42 equals 28, which is an even number. If this is not the case, add extra beads to the circumference to get a total that fits this formula. For example, if the actual circumference is 16 beads, this number is not divisible by 3. Add 2 beads to make the total 18; 18 divided by 3 equals 6; 18 minus 6 equals 12, which is an even number.

With these numbers established, thread

a size 15 needle with 2 to 3 feet of waxed thread. Leave a hanging thread and string the even number of beads just calculated. Wrap the thread with the beads around the widest point of the sphere and tie a square knot. Tighten the tension around the crystal and then tie an overhand knot. Remove this circle of beads from the crystal and place it around the tapered object (Figure 6-27). Space the beads evenly apart and bead upwards, from the wider portion of the object to the narrower portion.

To start the second row, push the needle through the first bead strung (#1a) and string another bead (#2a). Skip the second bead in the first row (#1b) and insert the needle into the third bead (#1c; Figure 6-28). Pull any slack out of the thread.

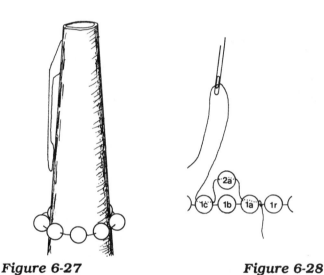

Figure 6-27   **Figure 6-28**

Continue to string new beads and anchor them to every other bead in the first row. At the knot, go down through bead #1a and back up through bead #2a (Figure 6-29). Notice that as the new beads are added, they push the beads skipped in the first row down, creating the appearance of three rows instead of two. If there are any gaps between beads or groups of beads, even out the distance between them so that there appears to be three beads in each spiral row (Figure 6-30).

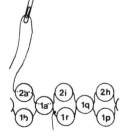

Figure 6-29   **Figure 6-30**

Move the circle of beads up to a slightly narrower section of the tapered object and string a new bead (#3a in Figure 6-31). Thread the needle through bead #2b and continue to add new beads between each of the raised beads from row #2. When the last bead is strung, insert the needle into the first bead of the second row (#2a) and up through the first bead of the third row (#3a). The easiest way to keep track of the rows and where they end is to count the beads in each one. Each row above the first row has half the number of beads that are in that base row.

Add row #4 in the same manner as row #3, then fit the crystal into the beadwork. Place row #1 at the widest part of the sphere (Figure 6-32). Finish beading two more rows of this half on the crystal. As in the Modified Comanche Stitch, this may not be easy. If the beadwork starts to slip, hold the sphere rather than the beadwork— this will help keep the beadwork on the crystal. Depending on the size of the crystal and the desired effect, more rows may be added to this half of the beadwork.

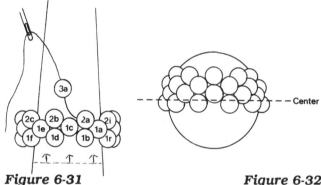

Figure 6-31   **Figure 6-32**

When the last row has been completed, insert the needle into the first bead of the last row and follow the spiral line of beads down to the bottom of the first row (Figure 6-33).

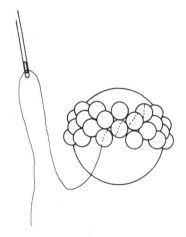

Figure 6-33

Without flipping the sphere over, string a row of beads (clockwise) between each lowered bead. Push each new bead into line diagonally and lock it into position by pulling the thread to the right (Figure 6-34). Count this as row #2 in the bottom half (the first being the lowered beads from row #1).

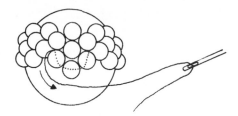

Figure 6-34

Continue the pattern by stringing rows #3-#6 as in the first half of the beadwork. When all the beads of the second half are strung, go through the bead that is next to the first bead in the last row and follow the spiral line of beads up to the center of the beadwork. Go through the center row and exit out of the next bead up the spiral row (the first anchor bead; Figure 6-35). String on six beads for an attachment loop.

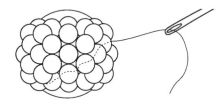

Figure 6-35

Using the same spiral row, skip the center row bead and enter the next bead down, from the bottom side (the second anchor bead). Continue through the center and first anchor beads and then go back through the loop beads (Figure 6-36). Weave the thread horizontally through the beads to the hanging thread, knot the two threads together, and hide them within the beadwork.

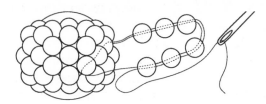

Figure 6-36

Drop-Sphere Earrings

As a variation for any beaded sphere earring, a single strand of beads can be attached to the top loop of a beaded crystal to create a drop earring. See Getting Started (Figures 1-20 to 1-24).

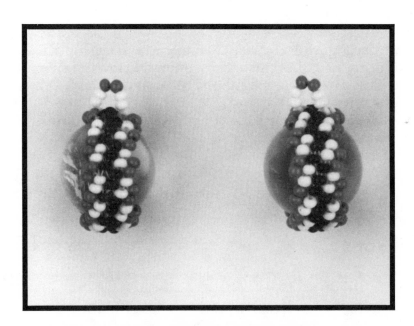

Three Drop Peyote Stitch in Black, White & Gray

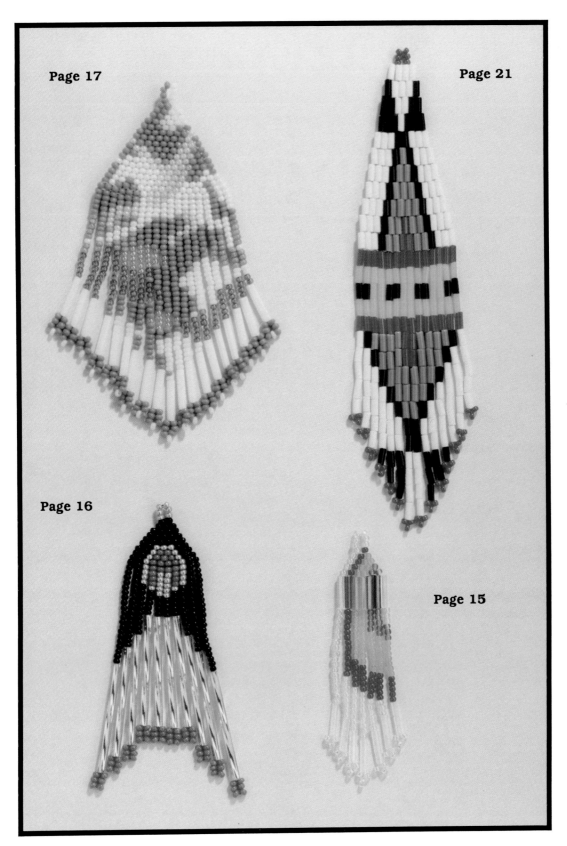

Page 17

Page 21

Page 16

Page 15

PLATE I

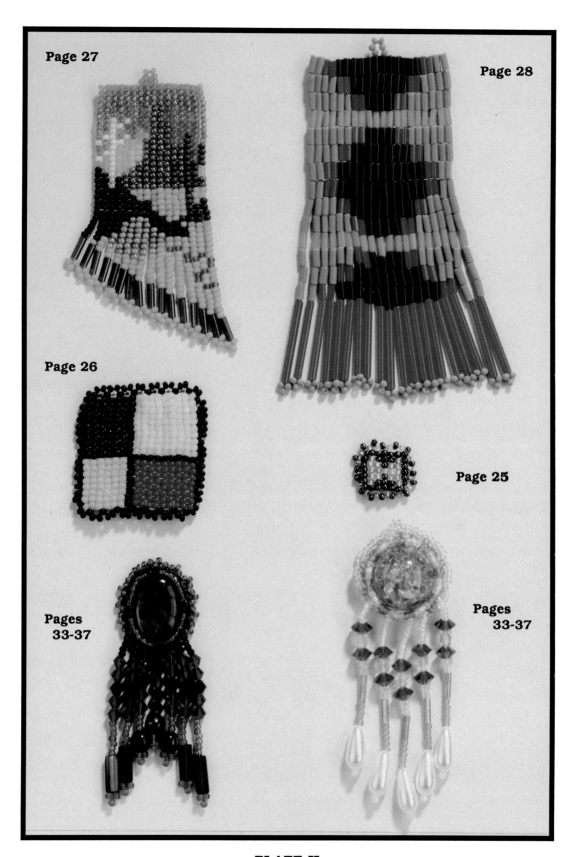

Page 27

Page 28

Page 26

Page 25

Pages
33-37

Pages
33-37

PLATE II

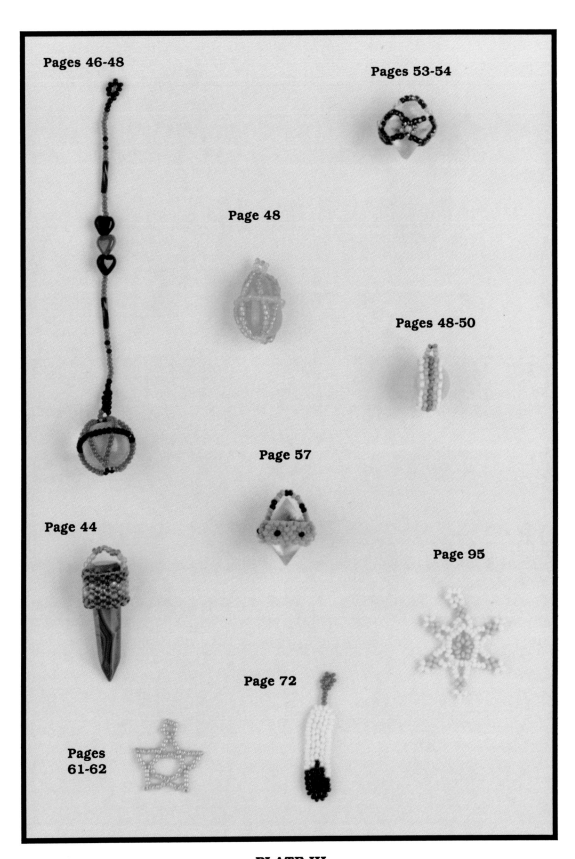

Pages 46-48

Pages 53-54

Page 48

Pages 48-50

Page 57

Page 44

Page 95

Page 72

Pages
61-62

PLATE III

Page 84

Pages 69-70
& Page 91

Page 80

Page 92

Page 85

Page 81

PLATE IV

BEADING FLUORITE CRYSTALS

Suggested Materials:

Size B Nymo Thread or Silk Thread
Size 15 and Size 16 Beading Needles
Size 13/° Seed Beads or Size 12/° 3-Cut Seed Beads
Matching Crystals

Fluorites naturally occur in a crystal form called an octahedron. This is an eight-sided shape which resembles two pyramids attached at their bases. The faces of the crystal may not be exactly the same size and must be measured before beading.

Modified Daisy Chain Stitch

This stitch creates a series of beaded flowers connected by strings of beads (chains) between the tops and bottoms of each flower. The beadwork is placed around the center of the crystal, with the chains above and below the corners and the flowers centered between the bases of the crystal faces.

Select two fluorites which have symmetrical sides and which match each other in size and color. Mark the top and bottom halves of each crystal with tape for later reference, making sure that any interesting features of the crystals are in the bottom half.

On the bottom of the crystal, measure with a string of beads from the center of one of the faces (A in Figure 7-1) to the center of the next face (B). Repeat this process from the center of face B to the center of face C. These are the numbers of beads to string between flower segments and often they will be the same.

If the distance between faces is different, alternate the two numbers between flower segments for the first chain. Use the same numbers on the second chain, but reverse the order (Figure 7-2). Note that it is not common for the distance between faces to differ by more than about one bead. If this is the case, it might be better to use a different crystal, rather than trying to adjust each chain segment so that the beadwork will fit properly.

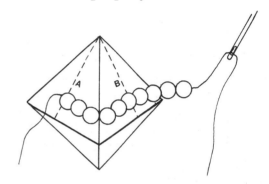

Figure 7-1

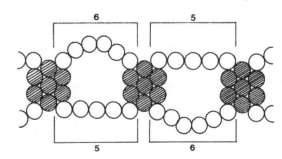

Figure 7-2

Thread a size 15 needle with about 2 feet of waxed thread. Leaving a hanging thread, string six beads of one color (#1 to #6) and enter back into the first bead strung (Figure 7-3). This will be the outside of the first flower. Keeping the flower beads tightly together, string a center bead of a second color (#a) and go through bead #4 from right to left. Go back through bead #a and through bead #1 from left to right (Figure 7-4).

String the number of chain beads previ-

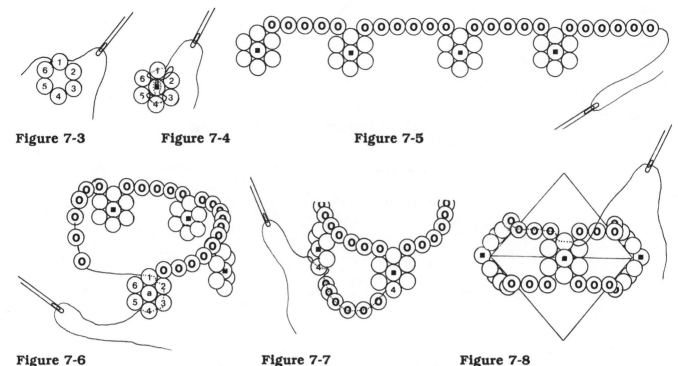

Figure 7-3   **Figure 7-4**   **Figure 7-5**

Figure 7-6   **Figure 7-7**   **Figure 7-8**

ously determined, using a third color, and then string a second flower as shown in Figures 7-3 and 7-4. Repeat the above steps until four flowers have been completed and string the last chain segment (Figure 7-5). To close this circle and begin the other side of the beadwork, insert the needle into bead #1 of the first flower segment. Continue clockwise through beads #2, #3 and #4 (Figure 7-6).

String the chain beads to connect flowers #1 and #4 (make sure the number is right), and push the needle through bead #4 of flower #4 (Figure 7-7). Continue stringing chain beads and threading the needle through the #4 beads of flowers #3, #2 and #1. Do not pull the thread tight. Flip the beadwork over (so the needle is at the top) and insert the crystal into the beadwork with the top half up. Position the flower segments in the center of each crystal face, midway between the top and bottom halves. Place the chains above and below the corners (Figure 7-8). Tighten the thread around the crystal.

String an even number of beads for an attachment loop— enough to reach the top of flower #3, plus enough to leave 1/8 to 1/4 inch between the loop and the top of the crystal. Take the needle through bead #4 of flower #3, from left to right (Figure 7-9). Go back through the loop beads and through bead #4 of flower #1, also from left to right. Pull the thread tight,

then run the thread through beads #5, #6 and #1, back to the hanging thread. Tie two overhand knots. Hide the main and hanging threads within nearby flower and chain segments and clip off any excess.

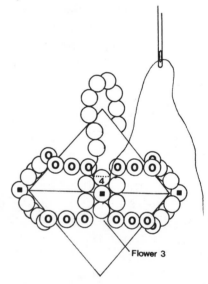

Flower 3

Figure 7-9

Modified Comanche - Patterns A to D

The Comanche Stitch can also be used to bead around the center of a fluorite crystal. Read the Comanche Stitch instructions (see Figures 2-1 to 2-14) before starting this project.

Measure the base of each crystal face with a Ladder Stitch gauge (see Figure 5-6); include the beads which overlap each corner in the measurements (Figure 7-10).

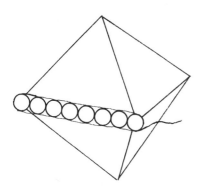

Figure 7-10

Using these numbers, select a pattern that will numerically fit the crystal. These patterns represent one repetition of the design for each of the faces of the crystal (four repetitions total). The single (outside) beads between the designs go around the corners of the crystal. If a simpler pattern is desired, try horizontal stripes. Use one color for the center row, a second color for the rows above and below it, and the first color for the top and bottom rows.

The beads outside each main design element can be added to, or deleted, to fit a specific pattern to a crystal face. Examples of patterns, including modifications, for crystal faces which are six beads long are shown in Figure 7-11. These are: two repetitions of the diamond (A) or daisy (B) pattern with no outside beads; one repetition of the chain pattern with no outside beads (C); one diamond (D) or daisy (E) with three outside beads; and one star with one outside bead (F). Figure 7-12 shows how to use two repetitions of a pattern and retain the outside beads between the design elements (in this case the crystal face is eight beads long). If the faces on a crystal are different sizes, add outside beads on the larger faces to cover the area.

When this row is complete, lay it around the circumference to ensure a good, snug fit (Figure 7-13). If it is too large or too small, redo it, adding or subtracting beads between elements as needed.

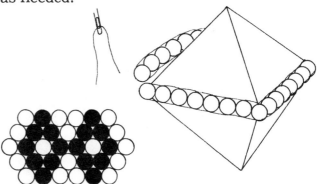

Figure 7-12   **Figure 7-13**

Remove the beads from the crystal. Connect the ends of the center row in the same manner as for spherical crystals (see Figure 6-18). Pull the thread tight and go back through the first bead strung (#1a). Flip the circle of beads, if necessary, so that the needle comes out the top of the beadwork.

Start the second row of beadwork with the regular Comanche Stitch technique (Figure 7-14). Continue adding new beads in a counterclockwise direction. The number of beads in each successive row on the crystal should decrease by one on each face, which requires skipping a bead. Do this at the corner of each face by skipping the thread between the two corner beads of the previous row. This places the first bead on the next face in the correct position (Figure 7-15). Pull the thread tight at each corner.

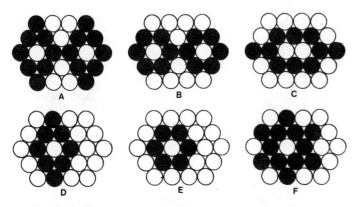

Figure 7-11

Thread a size 15 needle with 3 to 4 feet of waxed thread and Ladder Stitch the center row of the chosen pattern in one long line.

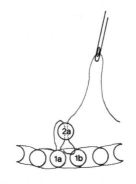 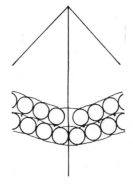

Figure 7-14   **Figure 7-15**

Connect the ends of the second row by running the needle down through bead #2a, under the threads between beads #1a and #1b, and back up through bead #2a (Figure 7-16). Pull the thread tight.

String the first bead of the third row and continue as in the second row. When the third row is completed, run the needle down through beads #3a, #2a and #1a (Figure 7-17).

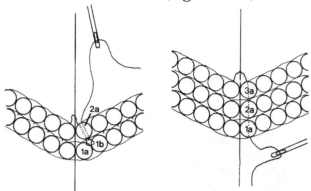

Figure 7-16   **Figure 7-17**

Flip the beadwork over, so that the needle is at the top, with the beadwork below the center row. Begin beading the next row (#4) above the center row, in a clockwise direction (Figure 7-18). Before connecting the ends of row #4, insert the crystal (top side up) into the beadwork with the center row at the junction of the top and bottom halves of the crystal (Figure 7-19). End row #4 in the same manner as row #2 and tighten the tension on the thread to hold the crystal in the beadwork. Bead the final row (#5) of the pattern. Finish this row by threading the needle down through bead #5a and then up through the last bead strung.

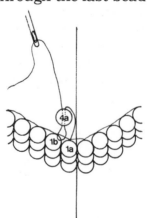

Determine the center bead(s) of row #5 on the last face beaded. If there are an odd number of beads in this row, there will be one center bead; if there are an even number of beads, there will be two center beads. Weave the needle and thread up and down through the beads in the top row to the center bead(s). The thread must exit out the **Figure 7-18** top of a center bead (the first anchor bead)— with an even number of beads on the face, this can be either of the center beads; with an odd number, if the thread enters the top of the center bead, continue down and run the needle under the threads from row #4, then bring the needle back up through the center bead (see Figure 7-16).

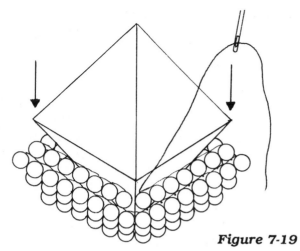

Figure 7-19

String enough attachment loop beads to go over the crystal to the beadwork on the opposite face with 1/8 to 1/4 inch between the loop and the top of the crystal. Use colors that are found within the beadwork.

Find the center bead(s) on the opposite face. If there are an odd number of beads in the top row, take the needle down through the center bead and continue down through the nearest bead to the left in row #4. Come up through the adjacent bead on the right and back through the center bead (Figure 7-20). If there are an even number of beads in the top row, go down through the center bead directly opposite the first anchor bead, and come back up through the other center bead in the top row (Figure 7-21).

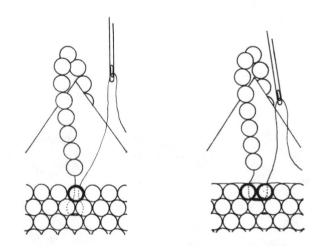

Figure 7-20   **Figure 7-21**

Take the needle and thread back through the attachment loop beads and go down through the center bead on the other side. If there are two center beads, enter the top of the center bead to which the loop is not yet attached. Tighten the thread, pulling the loop beads together over the top of the beadwork. Continue down through the beads to the center row and weave the thread around the crystal to the hanging thread. Tie the main and hanging threads together with two overhand knots and hide both ends by weaving them into the beadwork. Clip any excess thread.

Pattern A: Daisy

Pattern B: Diamond

Pattern C: Chain

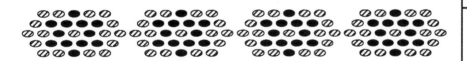

Pattern D: Star

Legend
Seed Beads
◑ = 13/o Turquoise
⊗ = 13/o Lt. Red
● = 13/o Black

Legend
Seed Beads
⊗ = 13/o Lt. Purple
⊘ = 13/o Lt. Pink
◐ = 13/o Turquoise

Legend
Seed Beads
● = 13/o Dk. Blue
⊗ = 13/o Med. Yellow
◐ = 13/o Med. Red

Legend
Seed Beads
⊘ = 13/o Lt. Pink
● = 13/o Black

NOTES:

FIVE NEW BEADED EARRING TECHNIQUES

This section contains five innovative earring techniques and variations. The first two techniques are fairly simple and quick to execute. The last three offer a challenge for the advanced beadworker and require familiarity with many of the basic techniques already described. These earlier techniques are combined in unusual ways to create earrings that are guaranteed to make any beaded earring aficionado stop and take notice.

BEADED STARS

Suggested Materials:

> **Size A Nymo Thread**
> **Size 13 and Size 15 Beading Needles**
> **Size 11/° or 13/° Seed Beads *or***
> **Size 12/° 3-Cut Beads**

Beaded stars can be made in either six-sided or five-sided styles. The completed size of the stars depends upon the size bead used. Use a single color for the first attempt at each earring style.

Six-Sided Star

Use a needle size appropriate for the size bead chosen and about 2 feet of waxed thread. String one bead (#1) on the thread. Leave a hanging thread and tie a single overhand knot around the bead (Figure 8-1).

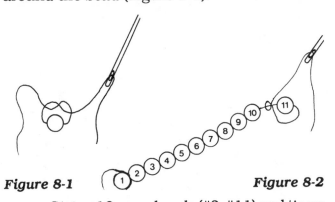

Figure 8-1   *Figure 8-2*

String 10 more beads (#2-#11) and tie an overhand knot around the last bead (Figure 8-2). To do this, separate bead #11 from the other beads and tie the knot loosely around the thread between beads #10 and #11. Hold the thread in one hand and insert the needle into

bead #11 (do <u>not</u> catch any thread on the needle). Use the needle to push bead #11 back towards the other beads, taking up the slack in the thread and tightening the knot when the beads are snug against one another (Figure 8-3).

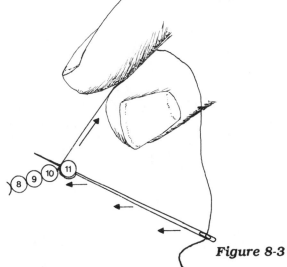

Figure 8-3

String another 10 beads (#12-#21) and repeat the procedure just described. There are now two sections of nine beads, separated by the tied beads #1, #11 and #21. To finish the triangular base of the star, string nine more beads (#22-#30) and run the needle back through beads #1-#4 (Figure 8-4).

59

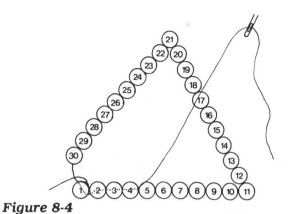

Figure 8-4

Add the three remaining outer arms of the star in a counterclockwise direction. To start, string four beads (#1a-#1d) and tie bead #1d with an overhand knot. String three more beads (#1e-#1g) and, skipping beads #5-#7 of the base triangle, go through beads #8-#10 (Figure 8-5). Pull the beads snug (forming a small triangle), so that no thread shows between them, but not so tight that the beads bunch together, ruining the triangular shape.

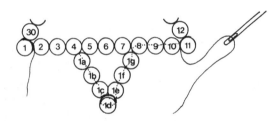

Figure 8-5

Skip bead #11 and run the needle through the next three beads of the base triangle (#12-#14). Repeat the procedure illustrated in Figure 8-5, stringing beads #2a-#2g and exiting out of bead #20.

Skip bead #21, go through beads #22-#24, and string beads #3a-#3g in the same manner as the other two small triangles. Exit out of bead #30 (Figure 8-6).

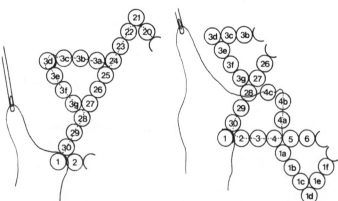

Figure 8-6   **Figure 8-7**

Connect the small outer triangles across the inside of the base triangle. To start, skip bead #1 and go through beads #2-#4. String three beads (#4a-#4c; Figure 8-7) and head clockwise through beads #27-#25. String three more beads (#5a-#5c; Figure 8-8).

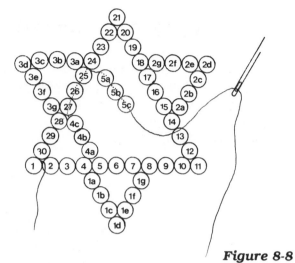

Figure 8-8

Go through beads #17-#15, string three more beads (#6a-#6c) and go through beads #7-#2 (Figure 8-9). Reinforce the star by going through all the outside star arms (skipping all the tied beads) and exiting out of bead #2 again (Figure 8-10).

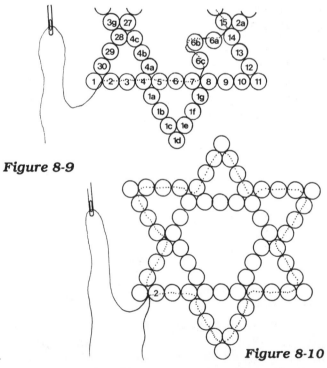

Figure 8-9

Figure 8-10

To make the attachment loop, take the needle through bead #1 and string six loop beads. Go back through bead #1 and through all of the loop beads again (Figure 8-11). Tie the main and hanging threads together, just below bead #1, using two or three overhand knots. Hide the thread ends and further reinforce the star by threading each end on a needle and going around through half of the outer star arms (one thread to either side, again skipping all tied beads; Figure 8-12). Emerge at beads #2c and #2e, respectively, and clip off any excess thread. Clear nail polish can be used to stiffen the star after the threads are hidden.

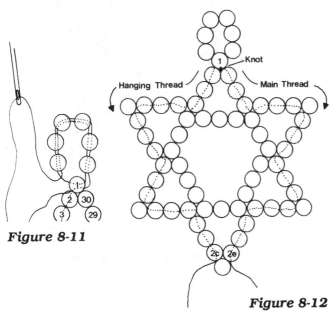

Figure 8-11

Figure 8-12

One variation of this design is to alternate colors within the star (Figure 8-13).

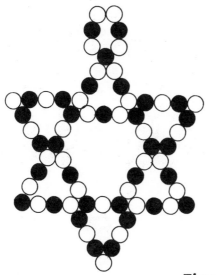

Figure 8-13

Five-Sided Star

Begin the five-sided star in the same way as the six-sided star (see Figure 8-1). After tying bead #1, string another 13 beads and tie

an overhand knot around bead #14. Then string 10 beads (#15-#24) and tie an overhand knot around bead #24. To complete the triangular base of the star, string 12 beads (#25-#36) and take the needle and thread through beads #1-#5 (Figure 8-14).

Begin constructing the rest of the star by stringing five beads to the outside of the triangular base (#1a-#1e). Tie an overhand knot around bead #1e, string four more beads (#1f-#1i) and run the needle counterclockwise through beads #9-#6 in the triangular base (Figure 8-15).

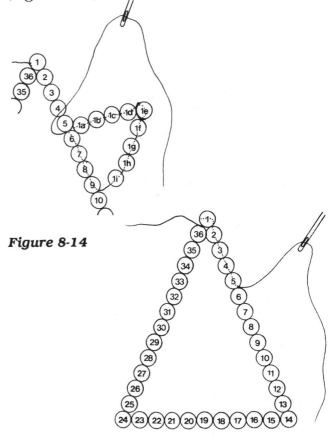

Figure 8-14

Figure 8-15

Next, string four beads across the inside of the base triangle (#2a-#2d) and go through beads #32-#29. String five beads to the outside of the base (#3a-#3e) and tie an overhand knot around bead #3e. String four more beads (#3f-#3i) and go counterclockwise through beads #32-#29 again (Figure 8-16).

Now string four beads (#4a-#4d) to the inside of the base and go through bead #19. String four more beads (#5a-#5d) on the inside and go through beads #9-#1 (Figure 8-17). Reinforce the star by running the needle and thread counterclockwise through all the outside star arms (skipping all tied beads and bead #19)

61

and exiting again out of bead #1 (Figure 8-18).

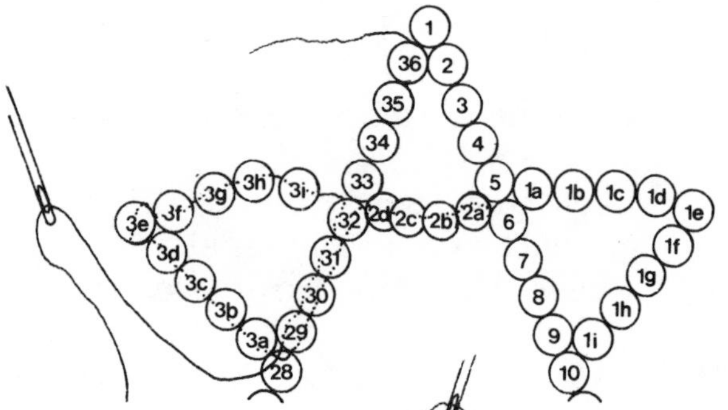

Figure 8-16

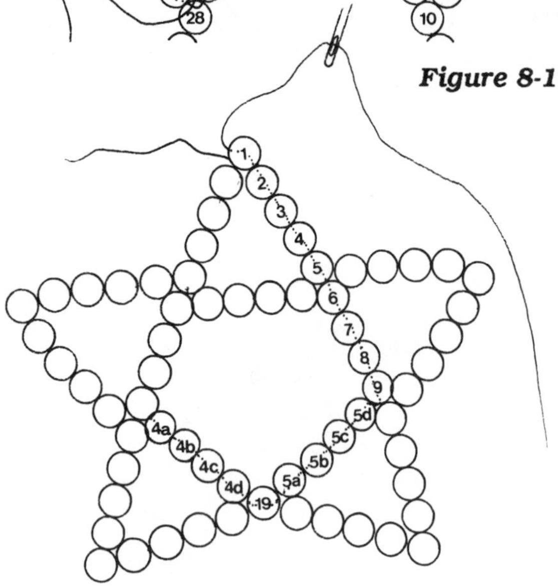

Figure 8-17

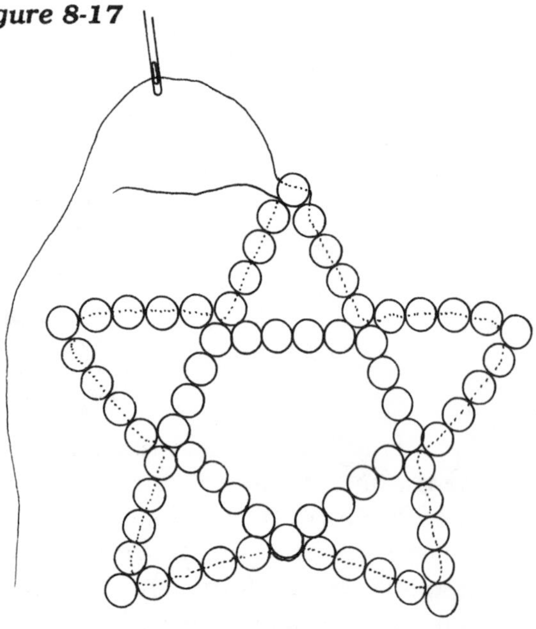

Figure 8-18

To make the attachment loop and knot the threads, follow the procedures for the six-sided star (see Figures 8-11 & 8-12). The only difference is that, when hiding each thread through half of the star, the main and hanging threads will both exit out of bead #19. Stiffen the star with clear nail polish if desired.

Alternate colors can also be used within the five-sided star (Figure 8-19).

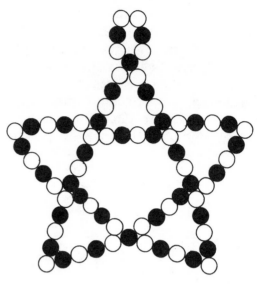

Figure 8-19

Both beaded star designs can be made bigger by increasing the number of beads. For example, start a six-sided star with 12 beads instead of 11 and add an extra bead to each triangular base segment, so that the total number of base beads is 33. Add an extra bead to each star arm segment (four beads in each segment, separated by a tied bead) and skip four beads between each outer star arm (Figure 8-20).

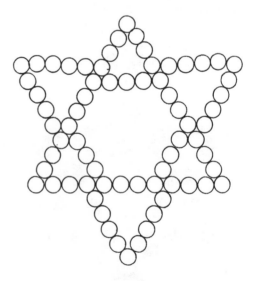

Figure 8-20

Drop earrings can be created by beading a star at the bottom of a single fringe element. Two or more drop stars can be strung together on a single earring (see *Getting Started*, Figures 1-20 to 1-24).

BEADED HEARTS

Suggested Materials:

> Size 11/° or 13/° Seed Beads *or*
> Size 12/° 3-Cut Beads
> 34 Gauge Beading Wire
> Needle-Nosed Pliers

In this earring technique, beading wire is used instead of thread to take advantage of its shape-holding abilities. Choose stainless steel wire and be careful, as some brands of wire tend to tarnish or even rust. Use wire cutters or scissors other than the ones used for beading to cut the wire. The length of wire needed depends upon the size and quantity of beads used. Generally, 1-1/2 to 2 feet should be more than enough. It is easiest to use a single bead color the first time this technique is attempted.

To start, string one bead and push it to the middle of the piece of wire. Tie an overhand knot around this bead (Figure 9-1); pull the ends of the wire evenly, keeping the bead in the center, until the knot is tight around the bead. Keep the wire as straight as possible while working with it, especially at the ends, because it is difficult to string beads on bent wire. When the knot is secure, bend the wire above the center bead into a V-shape (Figure 9-2).

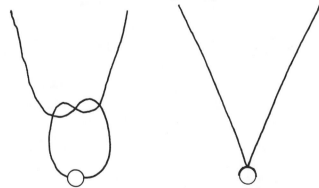

Figure 9-1   *Figure 9-2*

String the beads for the heart; the number to string depends upon the desired size of the finished heart and what size beads are

used. A good way to determine heart size is to start stringing beads on one half of the wire (Figure 9-3). Periodically bend this half into a heart shape and quit when the size looks right (Figure 9-4). Straighten the wire back into a V and string the same number of beads on the other half of the wire.

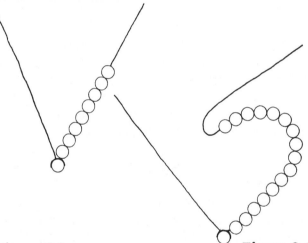

Figure 9-3   *Figure 9-4*

When both sides have the same number of beads, thread a single bead (the "base" bead) over both ends of the wire. Push the base bead down until it rests on top of the beads already strung (Figure 9-5).

Take a second bead (the "holder" bead) and again thread it over both ends of the wire. Push it down until it rests on top of the base bead (Figure 9-6). Keep the holder bead in position and thread one end of the wire back into the base bead. Pull slowly and evenly on the wire until it is completely through the base bead (Figure 9-7). Be gentle so that the beads don't break.

63

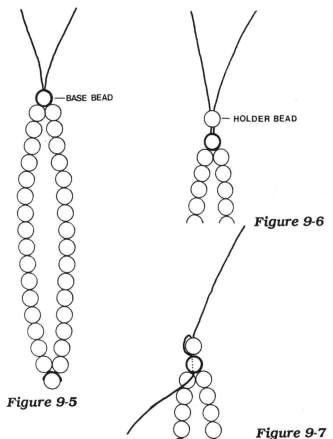

Figure 9-5

Figure 9-6

Figure 9-7

String four beads on each wire to make the attachment loop. Insert each end of the wire into the loop beads on the opposite side (Figure 9-10). Pull first one end and then the other completely through the opposing loop beads; avoid kinks in the wire and keep the loop beads as close to the base bead as possible.

Straighten out the heart and hide the ends of the wire by inserting them as far as possible down through the main beads on either side of the heart (Figure 9-11). It's helpful to use pliers to pull the wire down through the sides. The wire does not have to extend through all the heart beads, nor do the ends have to exit at the same place on either side of the heart.

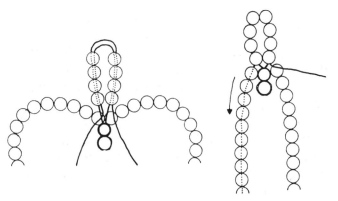

Figure 9-10   Figure 9-11

Push and pull the other end of the wire through the base bead in the same manner (Figure 9-8). Be careful not to let either wire kink while pulling it through the base bead. If this happens, pry the kinked loop open with a pair of pliers and then pull this section of the wire through the base bead carefully. Make sure the wires are all the way through the base bead and that all the beads are snug against one another.

Fold the top section of beads down, forming the top of the heart. The holder bead should point down towards the center of the heart and the ends of the wire should point up (Figure 9-9).

If the end of the wire gets lost, pinpoint its location by bending the heart at various points to see whether there are one or two wires between the beads. Once the end is located, bend the heart at a 90° angle, one bead below the wire's end. Push down on the top of the wire and grasp the end with the pliers (Figure 9-12).

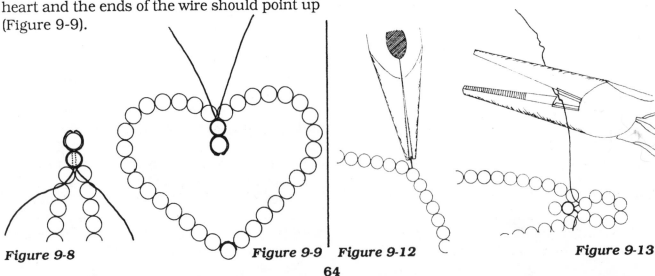

Figure 9-8   Figure 9-9   Figure 9-12   Figure 9-13

The end of the wire may become crimped during this procedure, in which case it will cease to travel through the beads. If this happens, pull the wire out of the heart section and snip off the kinked end (Figure 9-13). Then push the wire through the heart section beads again.

Bend the heart at a 90° angle where the wire comes out of it on each side (see Figure 9-12) and snip off the excess wire. Bend the heart back into shape (Figure 9-14). Cover the heart with clear nail polish if desired to further reinforce and hold its shape.

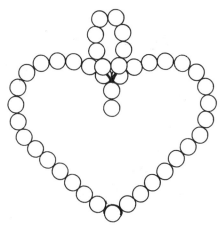

Figure 9-14

Beaded hearts can be varied in several ways. One adaptation is to alternate bead colors around the heart (Figure 9-15).

Figure 9-15

Another modification is to attach a cut-crystal heart, decorative bead, or other dangle in place of the holder bead (Figure 9-16). This requires more wire than the regular style. Attach the dangle carefully to avoid chipping or cracking it; leave a small amount of wire between the base bead and the dangle so that the

dangle will swing freely. Once the dangle section is folded down, pull on the wires with pliers to adjust the distance between the base bead and the dangle if necessary. When this is done, twist the wire within the base bead so that the dangle faces in the proper direction.

Figure 9-16

To attach a decorative bead with a vertical hole, string it between the base and holder beads. Then insert the ends of the wire back through the decorative and base beads, and continue the earring construction as normal (Figure 9-17).

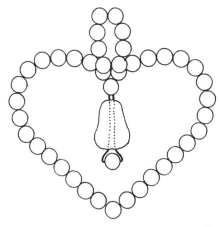

Figure 9-17

Single or multi-drop earrings can be made by beading the hearts first and using beading needles and thread to string the drop element(s) through the attachment loops (see *Getting Started*; Figures 1-20 to 1-22).

A final alternative is to create a lace heart with size 11/° seed beads. This variation also requires beading needles and thread. Start the heart in the normal manner and determine the number of beads to use on each side of the heart (see Figure 9-4). Then string one half of that number on each wire and bend the wires above the strung beads back towards the center bead. Mark the point on the bare wire which measures two thirds of the strung beads from the top (Figure 9-18). Attach the base and holder beads at the point marked on the wire (see Figures 9-5 to 9-8).

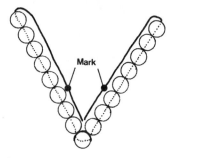

Figure 9-18

String a size 15 needle with about 1-1/2 feet of size A thread. Come up through the middle tied bead and leave a hanging thread. Add a single bead and take the needle through the next bead strung on the wire. String a single bead between each of the beads strung on the wire except for the two beads adjacent to the base bead (Figure 9-19). Add the attachment loop beads to the wire in the regular manner and hide the wires within the beadwork. Tie the ends of the thread together and hide them within the beadwork as well (Figure 9-20).

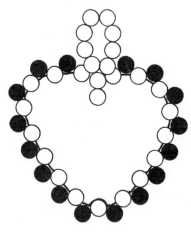

Figure 9-20

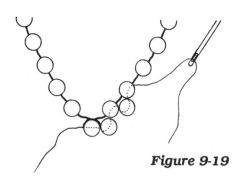

Figure 9-19

Red Beaded Heart

BEADED FEATHERS

Suggested Materials:

**Size 0 or A Nymo Thread
Size 15 and Size 16 Beading Needles
Size 13/° Seed Beads**

Beaded feathers are unusual in that the outside or perimeter of the earring is strung first and then the interior is filled with beads. The pattern described and illustrated is for a white feather with a black tip (see Pattern), but many other combinations are possible. Look at natural feathers and try to copy their designs or, if using the feather as fringe, use colors found in the main earring. These earrings were inspired by a pair purchased in San Francisco, California in 1985.

Feather Earrings

Thread a size 15 needle with 2-1/2 to 3 feet of thread. Begin the earring by stringing 44 beads for the outside or perimeter row. For this pattern, use 16 white beads, 12 black beads and 16 white beads. Leave a hanging thread and make a circle of the beads. Tie the main and hanging threads securely with two overhand knots. The use of the overhand knot allows for periodic adjustment of the perimeter bead tension.

Hold the beads so they form an oval, with the knot at the top center of the earring and the hanging thread on the left. To avoid confusion, always hold the beads this way. Keep the thread tension tight and insert the needle clockwise through the first bead to the right of the knot (Figure 10-1). String a single bead (#a) and push the needle counterclockwise through the first bead to the left of the knot (Figure 10-2). For this pattern, use all white beads in the top portion of the earring.

String a second bead (#b) and take the needle back through bead #a (Figure 10-3). String bead #c and loop the main thread around the thread between perimeter beads #2 and #3,

on the right side of the oval. Bring the needle back through bead #c (Figure 10-4).

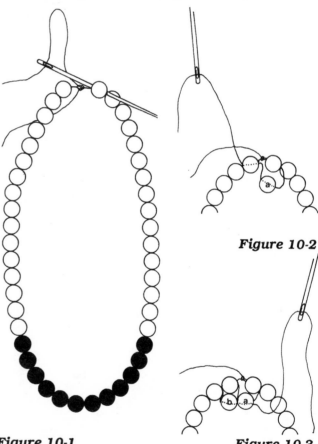

Figure 10-2

Figure 10-1   *Figure 10-3*

Keep pulling the main thread tight to maintain the tension on the center beads. Also pull on the hanging thread to maintain a tight tension on the perimeter beads. The tension on the perimeter can be adjusted later by pulling on the beads, but at this point it is important to keep the tension tight on both threads.

String another bead (#d) and go through bead #b (Figure 10-5). Go around the perimeter

67

thread between beads #2 and #3 on the left side of the oval and string bead #e (Figure 10-6). Go through bead #d and string bead #f. Go around the perimeter thread between beads #3 and #4 on the right, and then go back through bead #f (Figure 10-7).

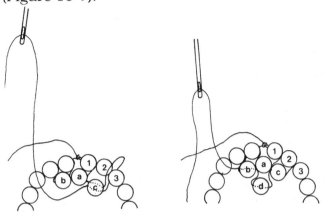

Figure 10-4   **Figure 10-5**

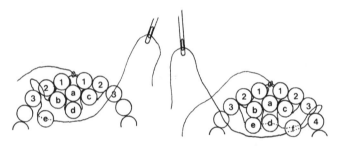

Figure 10-6   **Figure 10-7**

Notice that a pattern is emerging. On one pass, as the needle heads left, a middle bead is attached (Figure 10-8). On the next pass, as the needle heads right, two beads are attached which flank the middle bead (Figure 10-9). This process is actually a kind of flat Peyote Stitch, which is anchored on each side by the perimeter beads.

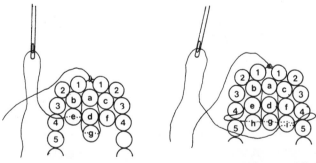

Figure 10-8   **Figure 10-9**

From this point on, simply repeat this two-pass cycle, moving down towards the bottom of the feather. Remember to periodically adjust the tension on both the perimeter and center beads.

The only other thing to be aware of is the possibility of having to skip perimeter beads when looping around the oval. Because the perimeter beads are positioned horizontally and the center beads are positioned vertically, it is necessary to periodically skip to the next perimeter bead down the line to make the loop around the perimeter (Figure 10-10). This prevents the center beads from bunching up and should be done if the spot on the perimeter where the loop attachment would normally occur brings the flank bead too close to the bead above it.

Start the black tip of the feather near perimeter beads #13 and #14 on the right side of the oval (Figure 10-11). String a black middle bead on the first pass of one of the two-pass cycles. On the second pass, flank this middle bead with two white beads (Figure 10-12). The remainder of the center beads, from this point down, should be black beads. Once the beaded feather technique is mastered, the design can be altered by changing the number of black beads on the perimeter and/or the placement of the black beads in the center of the feather.

Figure 10-10   **Figure 10-11**

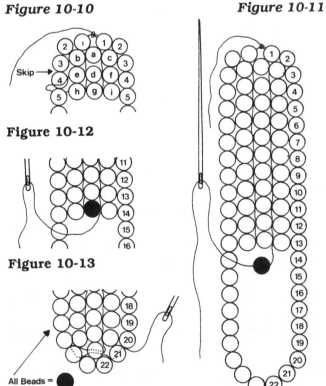

Figure 10-12

Figure 10-13

All Beads =

As the bottom of the feather is approached, perimeter beads may have to be skipped more often. A final middle bead should

68

be strung when the left and right flank beads are strung near perimeter beads #19 and #20. Attach this middle bead in the normal manner and go through the nearest perimeter bead on the left (approximately bead #21). Go back through the final middle bead and then through the nearest perimeter bead on the right (approximately bead #21; Figure 10-13). Continue up through the perimeter beads, counterclockwise, and exit at the top of the earring, by the knot and hanging thread (Figure 10-14).

Due to skipping perimeter beads, it may not be possible to end the center portion of the feather as described above. If there is not room for a final middle bead, attach the final left flank bead normally and then string the final right flank bead. To attach this bead, go through the nearest perimeter bead (do not make a loop around the perimeter thread) and continue up through the perimeter beads to the top of the earring (Figure 10-15).

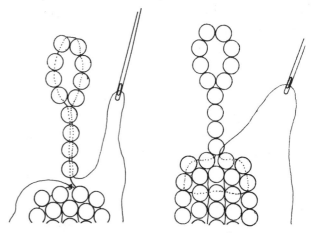

Figure 10-16   **Figure 10-17**

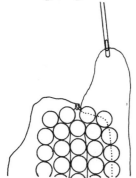
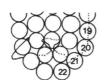

Figure 10-14   **Figure 10-15**

To create the attachment loop, string four red beads for the feather shaft and eight red beads for the loop. Go down through the "shaft" beads and exit at the knot (Figure 10-16). The red beads simulate the shaft of a feather wrapped with red trade cloth, a traditional Native American form of decoration.

To anchor the attachment loop, go down through the first two or three perimeter beads on the left and exit by a flank bead. Go through this flank bead and across the feather through the nearest middle and right flank beads. Enter the nearest perimeter bead on the right and continue up through the perimeter, counterclockwise, to the knot (Figure 10-17). Go up through the red beads again, then go through the eight loop beads twice for strength. Finally, go back down through the red beads to the knot (Figure 10-18).

Tie the main and hanging threads to-

gether with two or three overhand knots. To hide the main thread, go down through the perimeter beads to the left and weave the thread across to the right perimeter. Go down one row and weave the thread back across to the left (Figure 10-19). Hide the hanging thread in the same manner, but start to the right and weave the thread in the opposite direction. Clip any excess threads and coat the back of the feather with clear nail polish.

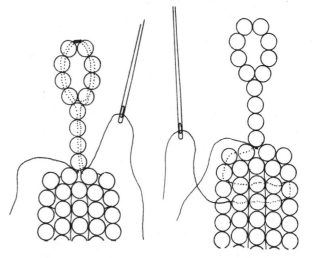

Figure 10-18   **Figure 10-19**

Feathers as Fringe

Beaded feathers, without the attachment loop, make attractive fringe additions on many different styles of earrings. They can serve as the only fringe elements or they can be added at the bottom of more complicated fringe designs.

Fringe feathers may be beaded as part of the main earring or they can be beaded separately and then added to an earring. In choosing between these two methods, the main consideration is the amount of thread required versus what can be comfortably handled. Thread for each feather must be added to the starting thread if the feather will be part of a main earring. If the main earring uses a lot of thread, or if there are several feather dangles to add, consider making the feathers separately and adding them to the main earring after it is completed.

To bead the feathers as part of a main earring, increase the starting thread needed for the project by 2 feet for each feather dangle. Bead the main earring style in the normal manner.

When ready to add the fringe, simply string the number and style of beads desired above the feather. If red beads, representing a cloth-wrapped feather shaft, are desired at the top of the feather, include these in the fringe beads strung at this time. Start the feather at the bottom of the fringe beads, using the instructions for the Feather Earrings. Be careful of the tension on the fringe beads when knotting the thread for the feather. When the feather is completed, run the thread back up through the fringe beads and continue as described for the main earring.

To add the feathered fringe separately, bead the main earring without fringe and knot and hide the threads. Calculate the amount of thread needed for the total number of feathers and fringe beads desired, including enough to weave through the beadwork after the ends are knotted. Tie this thread to the main earring, near the first fringe attachment point; be sure to leave a hanging thread to weave up through the main earring (see *Adding Thread* in *Getting Started*).

String the first set of fringe beads (including beads for a cloth-wrapped feather shaft, if desired), and start making the first feather. When the feather has been completed, go back up through the fringe beads and attach them as described for the main earring style. Position the thread to add the next fringe segment and string the next set of beads. Repeat these steps until all the fringe segments are completed, then weave the main fringe thread back into the main earring and tie a knot. Knot the hanging thread and hide both threads in the beadwork.

Feather Earrings With Circle and Cross

An interesting variation on the basic feather design is to bead a circle and cross design between the feather and the attachment loop. Any color combination can be used for the circle and cross. One suggestion is a yellow circle with a white cross.

Allow 2 feet of additional thread for the circle and construct the feather portion of this earring in the regular manner (see Figures 10-1 to 10-15).

After the thread is returned to the top of the feather, string two or three red beads (once again representing a cloth-wrapped feather shaft) and a single bead (#1) for the bottom of the cross. Run the needle back through cross bead #1, from bottom to top, and pull the thread snug (Figure 10-20). This will reposition cross bead #1 so that the hole is horizontal and the bead is secure on top of the red beads.

String four circle beads, a cross bead (#2), four more circle beads, a cross bead (#3), four circle beads, a cross bead (#4) and the final four circle beads. Change to a size 16 needle and go through cross bead #1, making a circle above the wrapped beads (Figure 10-21).

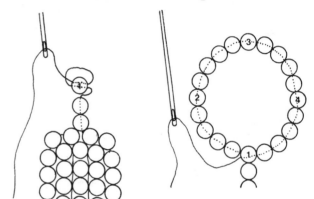

Figure 10-20   **Figure 10-21**

String five new cross beads (#a-#e) and go clockwise through cross bead #3 at the top of the circle. Go back down through beads #e-#a and clockwise through cross bead #1 again. Continue clockwise through the circle beads and exit out of cross bead #2, on the left side of the circle (Figure 10-22).

String two more cross beads (#f and #g) and go clockwise through bead #c. Go back through beads #g and #f and clockwise through cross bead #2. Continue around through the circle beads and exit out of cross bead #4, on the right side of the circle (Figure 10-23).

String the final two cross beads (#h and #i) and go clockwise through bead #c. Come back through cross beads #i and #h and clockwise through cross bead #4. Continue clockwise through the circle beads and exit out of cross bead #1 (Figure 10-24).

To reinforce the attachment of this upper section, continue down through the red cloth-wrapped beads and through one or two perimeter beads on the left side of the feather. Weave the thread across the body of the feather and then head back up through the right perimeter beads. Continue up through the red beads and exit out of the top red bead (Figure 10-25).

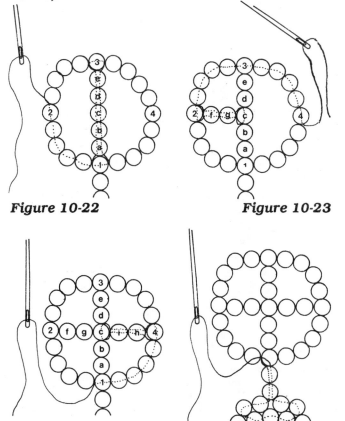

Figure 10-22   **Figure 10-23**

Figure 10-24   **Figure 10-25**

Skip cross bead #1 and go counterclockwise through the first circle bead to the right. Continue counterclockwise around the circle and exit just before cross bead #3 (Figure 10-26). The thread is now in position to add an attachment loop.

String eight loop beads and, skipping cross bead #3, enter the first circle bead to the left. Continue counterclockwise through cross bead #2, across through beads #f and #g, and then counterclockwise through bead #c. Continue across through beads #i and #h, counterclockwise through cross bead #4, and up through the circle beads, exiting just to the right of cross bead #3 (Figure 10-27).

To reinforce the attachment loop, skip cross bead #3 and enter the first loop bead on

the right. Go through all the loop beads, skip cross bead #3 and enter the first circle bead to the left. Continue counterclockwise through the circle beads and exit out of cross bead #1 (Figure 10-28).

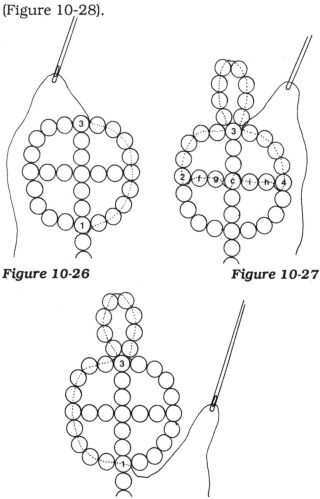

Figure 10-26   **Figure 10-27**

Figure 10-28

To finish the earring, go down through the red beads and securely knot the main thread with the hanging thread. Hide the main and hanging thread ends in the beadwork as described for the regular Feather Earring (see Figure 10-19).

Multi-Feather Drop Earrings

Another attractive style of feather earring features several feathers dangling from fringe segments of different lengths, all hung from a single attachment loop. The technique for making this variation is described in *Getting Started.*

Alternative Beads

In addition to regular seed beads, beaded feathers can be constructed using other types of beads, such as 12/° 3-cut beads or hexagonal beads. When working with these two types of beads it is important to remember that their shape affects the outcome of the feather. These two bead types are more "square" than a seed bead, so the number of perimeter beads must be decreased or the feather will be too long. Plan on using about 34 perimeter beads (12 white, 10 black and 12 white). Also, fewer perimeter beads will have to be skipped when attaching the flank beads. Be gentle when working with these beads and keep the thread well waxed, as their edges can be sharp and may cut or fray the thread.

Feather Pattern

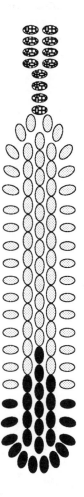

Legend
<u>Seed Beads</u>
◯ = 13/o White
● = 13/o Black
⬤ = 13/o Med. Red

Beaded Feather with Circle & Cross

72

BEADED FLOWERS

Suggested Materials:

Size O or A Nymo Thread
Size 13 and Size 15 Beading Needles
Size 13/° Seed Beads *or* Size 12/° 3-Cut Beads
Fringe Materials if Desired

The technique used to bead these earrings is a variation of the Comanche Stitch, similar to the version used for beading fluorite crystals. The major difference is that the faces or petals in the top half of the beadwork are not connected to one another. If unfamiliar with the Comanche Stitch or the variation used on fluorites, read the directions for these stitches (see Figures 2-1 to 2-20 and 7-10 to 7-19). It may even be helpful to complete a pair of beaded fluorites before attempting a pair of Beaded Flower Earrings.

Any of the Beaded Flower Earrings can be used to construct single or multiple drop earrings, as shown in *Getting Started* (see Figures 1-20 to 1-22).

Budding Flower - Patterns A to D

The "no fringe" patterns for this section show the beadwork as if it were one flat piece (similar to the patterns provided for the Comanche Fluorite Earrings). In actuality, the bottom portions of the beadwork will be joined into a flat, pentagon-shaped base, resembling the center of a partially opened flower. The upper portions of the beadwork will be arrayed at right angles around the base and appear as flower petals.

Thread a needle with approximately 3 feet of waxed thread. Start with the center row (the row which connects all five faces in the pattern) and Ladder Stitch the beads together, following the pattern for bead color and placement (Figure 11-1).

Fasten the ends of this row together in a circle (see Figure 6-18). Tie the main and hanging threads together with two overhand knots. Flip the circle of beads, so that the thread is at the top of the beadwork.

Bead the bottom half of the pattern first (the beadwork will be flipped back over later). Start the second row with a regular Comanche Stitch, beading in a clockwise direction (Figure 11-2). Remember to follow the colors for the bottom section of the pattern (the pattern may be easier to follow if it is flipped over so that the bottom section is at the top).

At the end of each face or section of the pattern, skip a bead in the center row to accommodate the decreasing number of beads (Figure 11-3). Pull the thread tight as each bead is skipped to form one corner of the pentagon. Connect the ends of the second row by running the needle down through the first bead in row 2, under the threads between the first two beads in row 1, and back up through the first

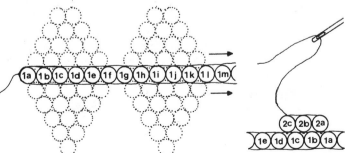

Figure 11-1   Figure 11-2   Figure 11-3

Figure 11-4

bead in row 2 (Figure 11-4).

Add the remaining rows of the bottom half in the same manner as the second row (Figure 11-5). Note that in the last (sixth) row, there is only one bead per face; therefore a bead in the fifth row must be skipped between every new bead added in the sixth. To complete this row, push the needle down through the first bead of the sixth row and continue down through the beads underneath it, exiting out the bottom of bead #1a (Figure 11-6). Flip the beadwork over so that the needle and thread are facing up.

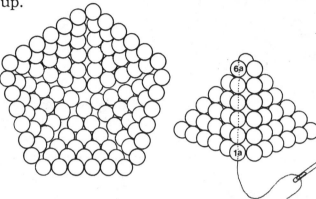

Figure 11-5   **Figure 11-6**

Bead the top half of the pattern next. Bead the first row of the top half employing the same bead-skipping technique used for the bottom rows. This will draw the top section together, matching the pentagon shape of the bottom.

Bead the remainder of each face separately. Make the inside of the pentagon the front of the beadwork, as this is the side which will be seen when the earring is finished. Start each new row with two beads instead of one, using the variation described for the Bugle Bead Comanche Stitch. Briefly, this involves stringing two beads and pushing the needle (from back to front) under the threads between beads #2 and #3 in the previous row. Bring the needle, from front to back, under the threads between beads #1 and #2, and go up through the first bead added (Figure 11-7). Pull the thread tight. Take the needle down through the second bead added, under the threads between the second and third beads in the previous row, and come back up through the second bead added. Finish the rows with the regular Comanche Stitch. Notice that each face ends with a row of two beads.

After the first face (petal) is beaded, turn the earring around to view the back side of this

petal. On the outside of the beadwork, insert the needle (from top to bottom) through the middle bead in the first row of the face (four rows from the top; Figure 11-8a). Pull on the thread to bend the petal backwards (Figure 11-8b).

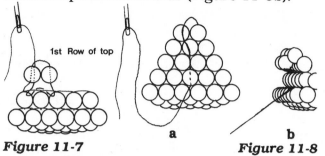

Figure 11-7   **Figure 11-8**

Weave the thread to the left, through the beads in the first petal row, to the first bead of the next petal section (Figure 11-9). Turn the earring around to view the inside of the flower. Bead the four remaining petals in the same manner as the first, remembering to keep the inside of the pentagon base as the front of the beadwork.

After beading and bending petal #5, thread the needle down to the right; go through the center row and through the fourth bead in the base row just below it (Figure 11-10). To add the attachment loop, string six loop beads and run the needle (from bottom to top) through the second bead in the same base row. Go back through the loop beads and through the fourth bead again, from top to bottom (Figure 11-11).

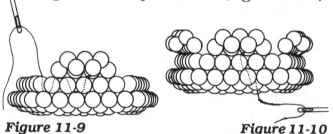

Figure 11-9   **Figure 11-10**

Weave through the beads to the hanging thread (Figure 11-12), tie the main and hanging threads together, and hide the thread ends within the earring. Wear the earrings with the bent petals facing forward.

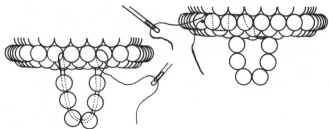

Figure 11-11   **Figure 11-12**

74

Blooming Flower - Patterns A to D

The same patterns (A to D) can be used to make Blooming Flower Earrings. The petals are flat in this version, rather than bent. Construct the bottom half of the pattern in the same manner as the Budding Flower Earrings (see Figures 11-1 to 11-6).

Bead each petal face of the top half separately, including the first row. (Do <u>not</u> use the bead-skipping technique for the first row as instructed for the Budding Flower Earrings.) Start each of these rows by stringing two beads as shown in Figure 11-7. At the top of petal #1, string six beads for an attachment loop. Go down through the top petal bead on the right,

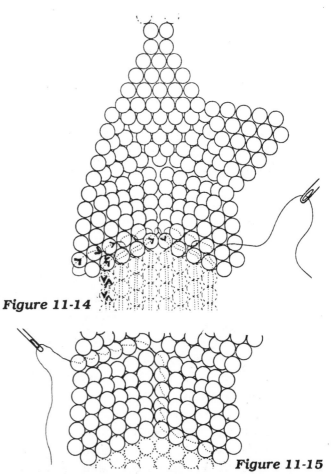

Figure 11-14

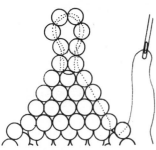

Figure 11-13

then up through the bottom of the bead on the left. Go through the six loop beads a second time and down through the beads on the edge of petal #1 to reach the first bead in the base row of petal #2 (Figure 11-13).

Continue in this manner, ending petals #2 and #3 with two beads at the top and exiting down through the edge beads (see Figure 11-13).

If fringe is desired, end petal #4 with two beads at the top. Do <u>not</u> go down through the edge beads. Orient the earring with petal #1 at the top and petals #3 and #4 at the bottom. Follow the pattern and add the fringe segments to the bottom edge beads of petals #3 and #4 and the center row beads between them. Work in a counterclockwise direction and anchor each fringe segment by going back up through the bead from which the segment originated and through the next petal bead above and to the right. Then go down through the next edge bead to the right, ready to add the next fringe segment (Figure 11-14). The two fringe segments at the junction of petals #4 and #3 are anchored through just the edge beads (see Figure 11-14).

To reach the starting point of petal #5, continue through the bottom edge beads of petal #3, then through the inside edge beads of face #3, to the center of the base pentagon. Go back out through the inside edge beads of face #5 to the center row, ready to add petal #5 (Figure 11-15).

Figure 11-15

Regardless of whether fringe is added or not, bead petal #5 in the same manner as the first four petals. Then run the thread down the upper edge beads of this petal to the hanging thread. Tie the threads with two overhand knots and hide the ends in the beadwork. Apply clear nail polish to the entire back of the flower to help keep the petals flat and hold the shape of the base. Avoid getting polish on the fringe segments, if any.

Daisy Flower Earrings - Pattern E

The center or base of this flower is constructed in the same manner as the previous two earrings, but it is made with six faces, instead of five, and there are only three beads in the base row of each face. This earring, unlike the Blooming Flowers, is completely flat. Familiarity with the Non-Loom Stitch (see Figures 3-1 to 3-13) as well as the Comanche Stitch and its variations is required to bead the petals. Although any two colors can be used, these instructions call for a yellow center and orange petal segments (see Pattern E).

Thread a size 15 needle with approximately 6 feet of thread. Following the technique used in the Budding Flower Earrings, Ladder Stitch 18 yellow beads together and connect the ends to form the center row (Figure 11-16).

Bead the remaining two rows of the bottom half with yellow beads, using the bead-skipping variation of the Comanche Stitch. After the last bead is added, thread the needle down through the edge beads of face #1 to arrive back at the center row (Figure 11-17). Flip the beadwork so that the needle and thread are facing up.

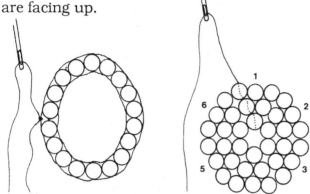

Figure 11-16   *Figure 11-17*

Bead each petal face of the top half separately, using orange beads. Bead the first row of petal #1, which consists of two beads (#1a & #1b), with the Bugle variation of the Comanche Stitch (Figure 11-18; see also Figure 11-7). Use the Non-Loom Stitch to add a second row of two beads; that is, string both beads (#2a & #2b) on the thread and go down through bead #1a. Come up through bead #1b and back up through bead #2a (Figure 11-19).

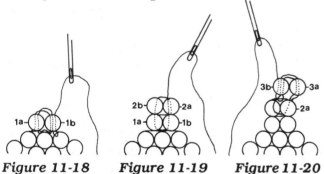

Figure 11-18   *Figure 11-19*   *Figure 11-20*

Row #3 has three beads and requires a new variation called the Comanche Add-On. String the first two beads (#3a & #3b) on the thread. Insert the needle under the threads between beads #2a and #2b, then go back through beads #3a and #3b. Go under the threads between beads #2a and #2b again, then back up through bead #3b (Figure 11-20). Add bead #3c using the regular Comanche Stitch. Attach this bead to the threads between bead #2a and #2b, the same attachment point that was used for beads #3a and #3b (Figure

11-21).

Attach the three beads of row #4 using the Non-Loom Stitch: string two beads (#4a & #4b) and go down through bead #3b; come up through bead #3a and add bead #4c; go down through beads #4b and #3b, and come back up through beads #3a and #4c (Figure 11-22).

Row #5 has four beads. Begin with the Comanche Add-On variation above bead #4c (see Figure 11-20). Add the remaining two beads with the regular Comanche Stitch, attaching both beads to the threads between beads #4a and #4b.

Add the four beads in row #6 with the Non-Loom Stitch (Figure 11-23). End with the thread coming out the top of bead #6c.

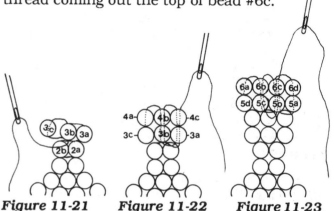

Figure 11-21   *Figure 11-22*   *Figure 11-23*

To bead row #7, which has three beads, start with the Bugle variation of the Comanche Stitch (see Figure 11-7). Starting from bead #6c does not change the way this stitch is executed. Add the third bead with a regular Comanche Stitch.

Bead row #8, which also has three beads, with the Non-Loom Stitch (see Figure 11-22).

Add the two beads in row #9 using the Bugle variation of the Comanche Stitch and then add the two beads in row #10 with the Non-Loom Stitch (Figure 11-24). String the last bead of the petal (row #11) and go down through bead #10b. Continue down through the beads on this edge of the petal and through the center base row bead of face #1 (Figure 11-25). Come back up through the next bead to the right (the edge bead in face #1), ready to start the second petal.

Complete petals #2-#8 using the same techniques as for petal #1 (see Figures 11-18 to 11-25). Bead petal #9 in a similar manner, except for the top row (#11). Attach this bead by going down through bead #10b, but then come back up through beads #10a and #11a.

String an additional six beads for an attachment loop and go back through bead #11a. Go through the six loop beads a second time (Figure 11-26), then go down through the edge beads of petal #9 (see Figure 11-25). Tie the main and hanging threads together and weave the ends into the beadwork. Clip off any excess thread, flatten the flower and stiffen it with clear nail polish.

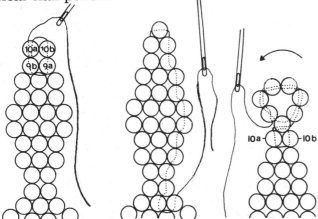

Figure 11-24   *Figure 11-25*   *Figure 11-26*

Rosette Flower Earrings - Patterns F-I

The center section of these earrings is constructed in much the same way as the previous flower earrings and consists of six faces with six beads in the base row of each face (Figure 11-27). Each of the patterns for this section also feature an optional fringe pattern. To incorporate the fringe, petals #6, #7, and #8 in the upper pattern must be deleted. Instructions for adding fringe (if desired) are provided in the next section.

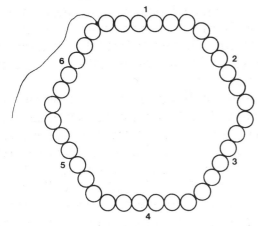

Figure 11-27

Thread a size 15 needle with about 6 feet of thread. Ladder Stitch the 36 beads in the base row together and connect the ends. Bead rows #2 through #5 using the bead-skipping variation of the Comanche Stitch.

In row #6, string three beads with the regular Comanche Stitch, without skipping any bead attachment points. Then skip one attachment point and string three more beads with a regular Comanche Stitch (Figure 11-28). Skip another attachment point and add the last three beads. Skip the final attachment point and go down through the first bead in row #6 again. Continue under its attachment point and back up through this first bead to position the thread for row #7.

String the first bead of row #7 and attach it as normal. Then skip two attachment points and add the second bead; skip two more attachment points, add the third bead, and push the needle down through the first bead in row #7 again (Figure 11-29). Run the needle through the edge beads on the left side of face #1 and exit out the first base bead.

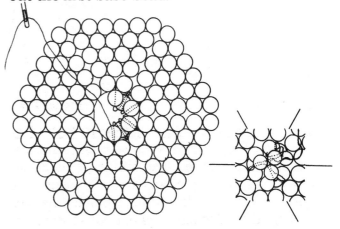

Figure 11-28   *Figure 11-29*

The petal construction for these earrings is simpler than for the Daisy Flower Earrings, because there is no Non-Loom Stitch beyond the first row. Note that there are 12 petals, one in the middle of each face and one on each of the corners between faces.

Add the first two beads of petal #1 (row #1) above the corner beads of faces #1 and #6, using the Non-Loom Stitch (Figure 11-30).

Attach the first two beads of row #2 with the Comanche Add-On variation and add the last bead in this row with a regular Comanche Stitch (see Figures 11-20 and 11-21).

Bead row #3 with the Comanche Add-On variation and two regular Comanche stitches. Use the attachment point between the last two beads in row #2 for both regular Comanche stitches.

Bead rows #4 and #5 using the regular

Comanche Stitch with the Bugle variation for the first two beads in each row. End this petal with a single bead at the top and an attachment loop of six beads (see Figure 11-26). Go down through the petal as shown in Figure 11-31, exiting out the first bead in the base row. Weave through the beads in the base row to the fourth bead in face #1. The needle is now in position to add petal #2.

Bead petals #2-12 using the same techniques as for petal #1. When petal #12 is complete, go down to the base row and weave through the beads to the hanging thread. Knot the two threads together and hide the ends within the beadwork. Stiffen the flower and petals with nail polish.

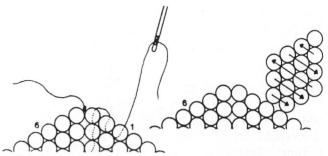

Figure 11-32   **Figure 11-33**

For all other patterns, construct the first five petals in the same way as for the previous Rosette Flowers. After exiting petal #5 and entering the base row, come out through the next base row bead in face #3 (Figure 11-34). This positions the thread for the first fringe element. This starting bead is different for the Blackfoot Fringe design, but the starting position is clearly shown in Pattern J.

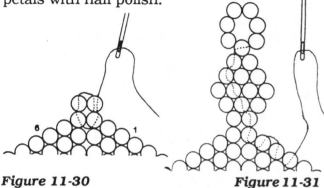

Figure 11-30   **Figure 11-31**

Rosette Flowers w/Fringe- Patterns J-K

Any of the Rosette Flower patterns can be made with fringe. The fringe provides an opportunity to use other materials such as bugle beads, porcupine quills, small feathers or feather fluffs. The earrings are constructed in the same way, except that fringe replaces petals #6 to #8.

Patterns J and K show where these petals are deleted. To bead these patterns without fringe, simply add three more petals in the missing space. Note that the starting point of petal #1 in Pattern J (Blackfoot Fringe) is in the middle of face #1 instead of at the corner. Many alternatives to the suggested fringe designs are possible. Begin with the colors found within the flower and be creative.

Start with a size 15 needle and about 10 feet of thread. Construct the bottom faces of the hexagon base in the normal manner.

For Pattern J weave the thread through the base row to the third bead in face #1 (Figure 11-32). Because of the starting point, the rows in this petal are constructed in the opposite direction from all the other petals (Figure 11-33).

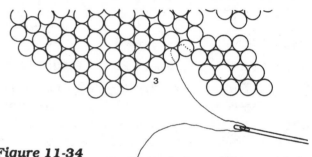

Figure 11-34

Add a fringe element to each of the 10 base row beads specified in the pattern, following the chosen fringe design. String the beads after the bugle bead in Pattern K as illustrated in Figure 11-35. If using feathers at the bottom of the fringe (as in Pattern J), do not worry about attaching them at this time. Note that bottom beads are required below the bugle beads to which feathers will be attached. In Pattern J, these are partially seen behind the feathers and are the same as for the middle, unfeathered fringe segments.

After completing the final fringe segment, exit out of the next base row bead to the left and continue the construction of petals #6-#9. The construction of petal #6 will be from the opposite side as illustrated in Figure 11-33. The exit from this petal is slightly different; go down through the edge beads closest to petal #1 (Figure 11-36). The remainder of the earring construction is the same as for the other Rosette Flowers.

To knot the threads in Pattern J, exit the bottom of petal #9 in the normal manner, but do not enter the base row. Knot the main and

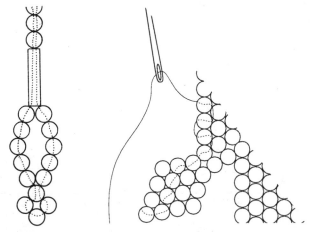

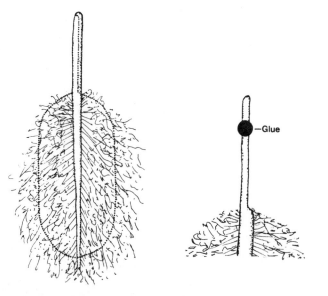

a bugle bead near the base of each fringe. Place a small drop of glue on the top part of the quill and insert it into the bugle bead (Figure 11-38).

Figure 11-35

Figure 11-36

hanging threads and hide the ends within the beadwork.

To add feathers, use small one inch feathers, or trim small fluff feathers to shape with a scissors (Figure 11-37). Trim the width and length of the quill portion of the feather, if necessary, so that it can be easily inserted into

Figure 11-37

Figure 11-38

Pattern A: Pink Budding/Blooming Flower
Without Fringe

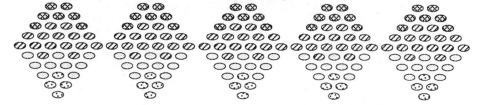

With Fringe

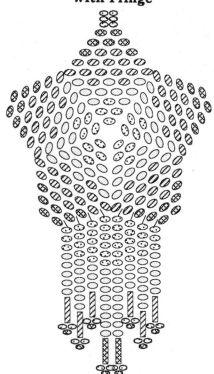

Legend
Seed Beads
⊘ = 13/o Lt. Pink
⊗ = 13/o Lt. Purple
○ = 13/o White
⊙ = 13/o Lt. Yellow
Bugle Beads
▨ = #5 (11mm) Lt. Pink
▩ = #5 (11mm) Lt. Purple

Pattern B: Purple Budding/Blooming Flower   Pattern C: Red Budding/Blooming Flower
Without Fringe

With Fringe

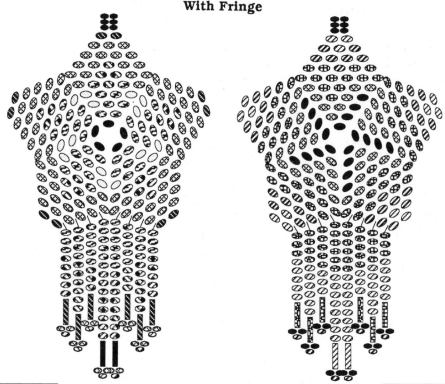

Legend		Legend

Legend

Seed Beads
⊗ = 13/o Lt. Purple
◔ = 13/o Dk. Purple
◕ = 13/o Dk. Blue
◑ = 13/o Orange
○ = 13/o White
● = 13/o Black

Bugle Beads

▨ = #5 (11mm) Dk. Blue

▮ = #5 (11mm) Black

Legend

Seed Beads
⊛ = 13/o Med. Red
⊘ = 13/o Dk. Pink
⊘ = 13/o Lt. Pink
⊗ = 13/o Lt. Purple
● = 13/o Black

Bugle Beads

▨ = #5 (11mm) Med. Red

▨ = #5 (11mm) Lt. Pink

Pattern D: Blue Budding/Blooming Flower
Without Fringe

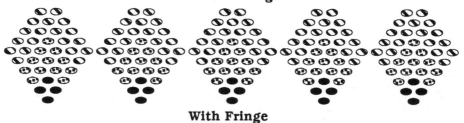

With Fringe

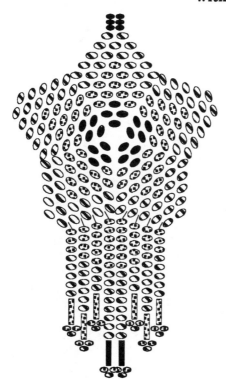

Legend
Seed Beads
👁 = 13/o Med. Blue
⊕ = 13/o Dk. Yellow
● = 13/o Black
Bugle Beads
▯ = #5 (11mm) Dk. Yellow
▮ = #5 (11mm) Black

Pattern E: Daisy Flower

Legend
Seed Beads
☺ = 13/o Lt. Yellow
✺ = 13/o Orange

81

Pattern F: Tri-Star Rosette Flower

Without Fringe

With Fringe

Legend

Seed Beads
- 😊 = 13/o Lt. Blue
- 😊 = 13/o Orange
- 😊 = 13/o Lt. Yellow
- 😊 = 13/o Med. Red

Bugle Beads
- ▤ = #3 (7mm) Orange

- ▥ = #5 (11mm) Lt. Blue

(Note: The fringe is an option. If no fringe is desired, continue adding three more petals in the fringe area.)

Pattern G: Quilt Rosette Flower

Without Fringe

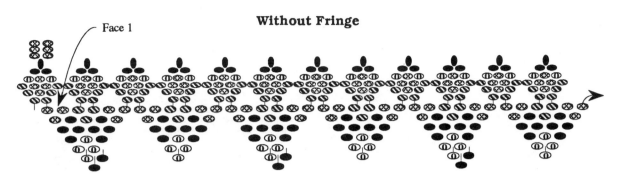

Face 1

With Fringe

Face 1

Legend
Seed Beads
⊗ = 13/o Lt. Purple
⊗ = 13/o Med. Blue
● = 13/o Black
⊕ = 13/o Lt. Red
Bugle Beads
▧ = #3 (7mm) Med. Blue
▮ = #5 (11mm) Black
(Note: The fringe is an option. If no fringe is desired, continue adding three more petals in the fringe area.)

Pattern H: Whirlwind Rosette Flower

Without Fringe

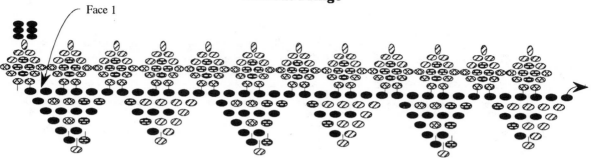

Face 1

With Fringe

Face 1

Legend

Seed Beads
- ● = 13/o Black
- ⊗ = 13/o Lt. Purple
- ⊖ = 13/o Lt. Blue
- ⊘ = 13/o Lt. Pink

Bugle Beads
- ▓ = #3 (7mm) Lt. Purple
- ▨ = #5 (11mm) Lt. Pink

(Note: The fringe is an option. If no fringe is desired, continue adding three more petals in the fringe area.)

Pattern I: Rainbow Rosette Flower

Without Fringe

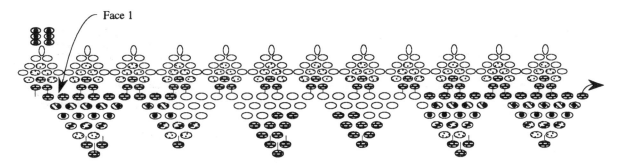

Face 1

With Fringe

Face 1

Legend	
Seed Beads	
⬌ =	13/o Lt. Blue
⬌ =	13/o Dk. Purple
⬌ =	13/o Med. Red
⬌ =	13/o Orange
⬌ =	13/o Lt. Yellow
◯ =	13/o Clear
Bugle Beads	
▯ =	#3 (7mm) Lt. Yellow
▮ =	#5 (11mm) Med. Red

(Note: The fringe is an
option. If no fringe is
desired, continue adding
three more petals in the
fringe area.)

Pattern J: Blackfoot Fringe

Rosette Flower With Fringe

Face 1

Fringe Area

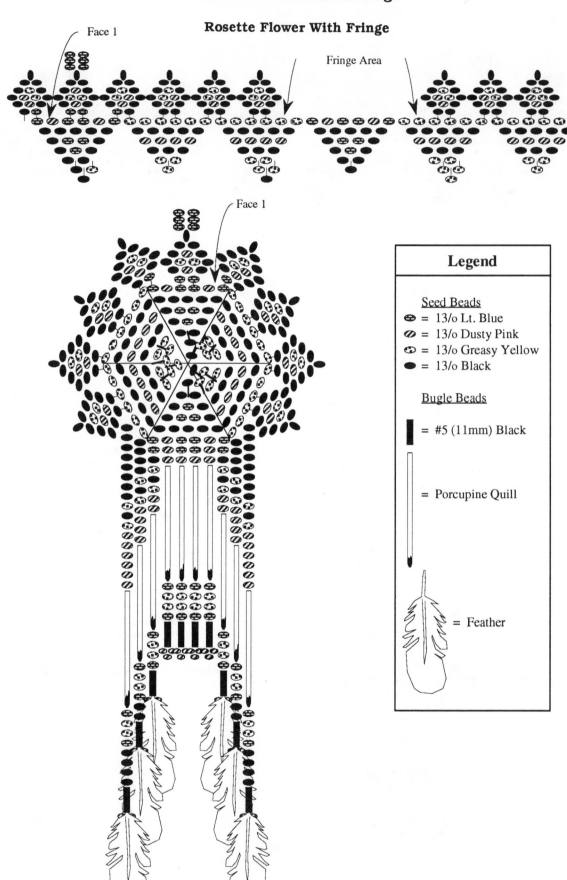

Face 1

Legend

Seed Beads

⊛ = 13/o Lt. Blue
⊘ = 13/o Dusty Pink
⊕ = 13/o Greasy Yellow
● = 13/o Black

Bugle Beads

▮ = #5 (11mm) Black

▏ = Porcupine Quill

= Feather

Pattern K: Peace Fringe

Rosette Flower With Fringe

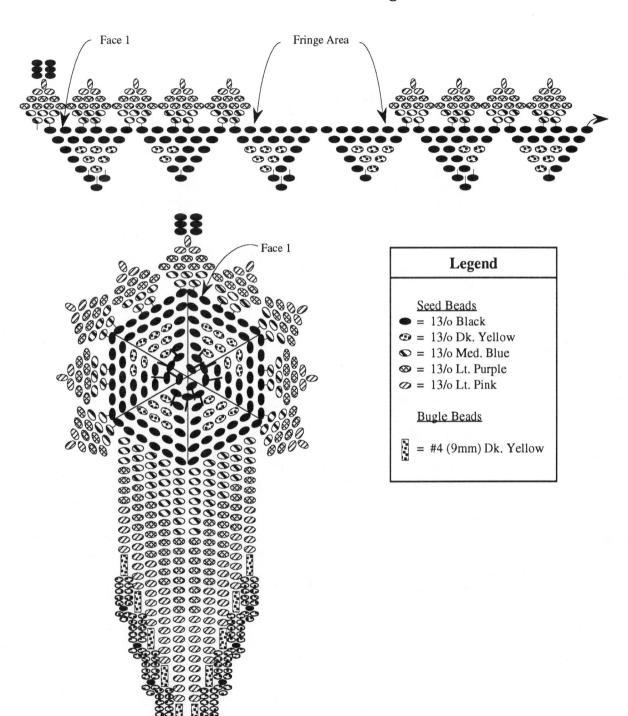

Face 1

Fringe Area

Face 1

Legend

Seed Beads

- ● = 13/o Black
- ◕ = 13/o Dk. Yellow
- ◒ = 13/o Med. Blue
- ⊗ = 13/o Lt. Purple
- ⊘ = 13/o Lt. Pink

Bugle Beads

▓ = #4 (9mm) Dk. Yellow

BEADED ROSETTES

Suggested Materials:

Size A or 0 Nymo Thread
Size 15 and Size 16 Beading Needles
Size 13/° Seed Beads *or* Size 12/° 3-Cut Beads
Fringe Materials as Desired

This technique creates beadwork similar to the rosettes produced by stitching beads to material, but in this case no backing is required. These earrings were inspired by a pair purchased in Reno, Nevada in 1984.

Four-Bead Rosettes - Pattern A

Accompanying Pattern A is a diagram showing bead number placement in a Four-Bead Rosette Earring. This diagram can also be used as a graph to design other Four-Bead Rosette Earrings. In this first set of instructions, the color of each row of beads is indicated to aid in reading and executing the pattern; refer to both the pattern and the diagram often. Because of the number of rows and the intricacy of the design the rows are designated 1, a, 2, b, etc., rather than 1, 2, 3, 4, etc. Bead designations within a row remain as a, b, c, d, etc.

Thread a size 15 needle with about 3 feet of thread. String five beads on the thread (beads #1a to #1e; black in Pattern A) and leave a hanging thread. Make a circle of the beads, and knot the main and hanging threads securely with a square knot (Figure 12-1). Go through all five beads again to strengthen the base, exiting from bead #1e by the knot.

All the beads in the second row (row #a) of the pattern are yellow. String a single bead (#aa) and put the needle through bead #1a; string another bead (#ab) and put the needle through bead #1b; string a third bead (#ac) and put the needle through bead #1c; string a fourth bead (#ad) and put the needle through bead #1d; string a fifth and final bead (#ae) and put the needle through bead #1e. Run the needle back through bead #aa to complete the row (Figure 12-2).

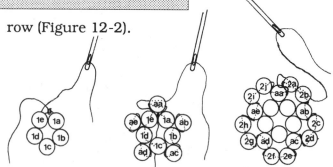

Figure 12-1   *Figure 12-2*   *Figure 12-3*

The beads in the next row or pass around the circle (row #2) are black in Pattern A. String two beads (#2a and #2b) and put the needle through bead #ab; string another two beads (#2c and #2d) and put the needle through bead #ac; string two more beads (#2e and #2f) and put the needle through bead #ad; string another two beads (#2g and #2h) and put the needle through bead #ae; string a final two beads (#2i and #2j), put the needle through bead #aa and then through beads #2a and #2b (Figure 12-3).

Note the above sequence, which illustrates the repetitive steps used in this technique. The beads strung on a given pass or row are subsequently used to anchor the beads strung on the next pass, and the number of beads per stitch increases by one after every two passes.

For the next pass (row #b), the beads in Pattern A are pink. String two beads (#ba and #bb) and put the needle through beads #2c and #2d. Continue stringing two new beads (pink) between each of the previous pairs of beads (black), until the last two beads in this pass (#bi and #bj) have been strung. Then put the needle

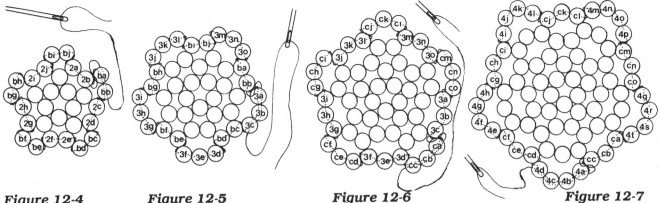

Figure 12-4   **Figure 12-5**   **Figure 12-6**   **Figure 12-7**

through beads #2a and #2b and back through beads #ba and #bb (Figure 12-4).

This time string three beads at a time; the beads in this pass (row #3) are again black. String beads #3a-#3c and put the needle through beads #bc and #bd. Continue stringing three beads (black) between each of the previous pairs of beads (pink), until beads #3m-#3o have been strung. Then put the needle through beads #ba and #bb and also through the first set of three beads, #3a-#3c (Figure 12-5).

Still following Pattern A, the beads in the next pass (row #c) are blue. String the first three beads (#ca-#cc) and put the needle through the beads #3d-#3f (black). Continue stringing three new beads (blue) between each of the previous sets of three beads (black), until beads #cm-#co have been strung. Then put the needle through beads #3a-#3c (black) and continue through the first set of new beads, #ca-#cc (Figure 12-6).

String four beads at a time in the next pass (row #4). In the pattern, these beads are black. String beads #4a-#4d and put the needle through beads #cd-#cf (blue). Continue string-ing sets of four beads (black) between each of the previous sets of three beads (blue) until the last four beads (#4q-#4t) have been strung. Then put the needle through beads #ca-#cc (blue) and also through the first set of four beads, #4a-#4d (Figure 12-7).

Again, string four beads at a time in this pass (row #d). In the pattern, these beads are purple. String beads #da-#dd and put the needle through beads #4e-#4h (black). Con-tinue stringing new sets of four beads (purple) between the previous sets of four beads (black) until beads #dq-#dt have been strung. Then put the needle through beads #4a-#4d (black) and also through the first set of new beads, #da-#dd (Figure 12-8).

For the last two passes (rows #5 & #e) string only four beads in each set, instead of progressing to five. Select beads for these passes which are fairly thick in comparison to the previous beads. This will balance out the use of four beads instead of five in these rows. The edges of the earring will tend to curl inward. This is to be expected and adds a slightly sculptured quality to the earrings.

The beads in row #5 are black in Pattern A. String beads #5a-#5d and put the needle through beads #de-#dh (purple). Continue stringing new sets of four beads (black) between the previous sets of four beads (purple) until the last four beads, #5q-#5t, have been strung. Then put the needle through beads #da-#dd (purple) and back through the first set of new beads, #5a-#5d (Figure 12-9).

For the last pass (row #e), string one black, two purple and one black bead in each set. String beads #ea-#ed and put the needle through beads #5e-#5h (black). Continue stringing new sets of four beads (in the sequence just given) between the previous sets of four beads (black) until beads #eq-#et have been strung (Figure 12-10).

Put the needle through beads #5a-#5d (black) and back through beads #ea-#ed. Continue clockwise around the perimeter of the earring, passing through all the beads in rows #5 and #e until bead #eo is reached. Exit between beads #en and #eo (purple) in the next to last set of beads in row #e (Figure 12-11). Orient the earring so that the needle and thread are on the bottom, right side of the rosette.

Attach the bead fringe and dentalium shells next. Details on preparing and working with dentalium shells are provided in the *Other Materials* section of *Getting Started*.

With the needle in position (see Figure 12-11), string the beads for the first fringe

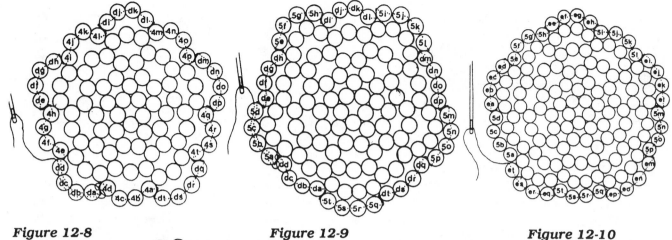

Figure 12-8

Figure 12-9

Figure 12-10

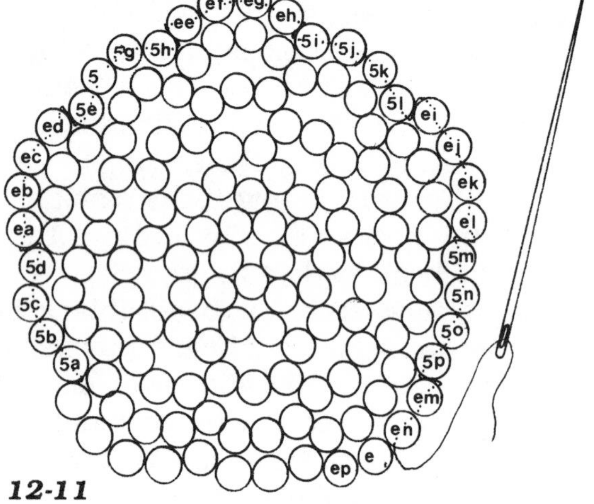

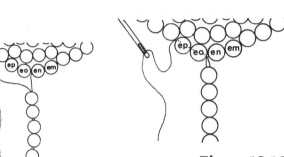

Figure 12-11

segment. Add one dentalium shell and a single white or clear anchor bead. The anchor bead must be small enough to fit inside the shell (13/° or smaller). Go back up through the shell and then through the rest of the fringe beads (Figure 12-12). Go clockwise through the next two beads in the perimeter of the earring (#eo and #ep) and emerge ready to start the second fringe (Figure 12-13).

All of the fringe segments are constructed in exactly the same manner, using the same number and sequence of beads and dentalium shells. Position the thread for each new segment by passing the needle clockwise through the next two perimeter beads to the left (Figure 12-14).

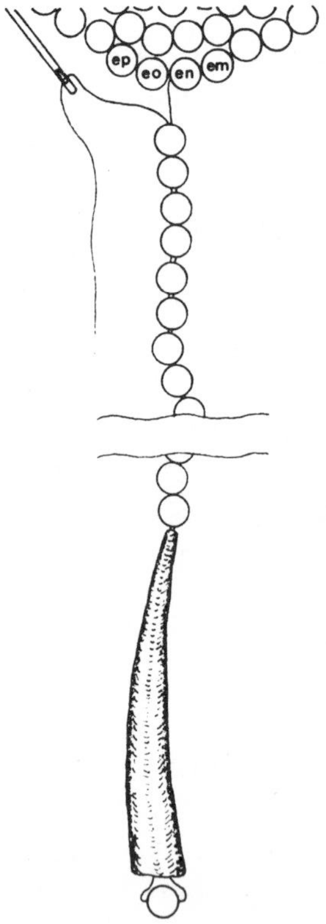

Figure 12-12

Figure 12-13

Anchor the last (fifth) fringe segment by passing the needle through the next two perimeter beads to the left. Moving inward, thread the needle clockwise through the sets of beads in each successive row, until the first row is reached. Enter the nearest bead (black) in the first row and continue around to the hanging thread. Exit out of bead #1e and knot the main thread with the hanging thread (Figure 12-15).

Hide the main thread in the beadwork, following the sets of beads in each row clockwise, back out towards the perimeter. Exit at about the fourth row (row #b) and cut the main thread (Figure 12-16). Hide the hanging thread in the same manner.

To complete the earring, attach the finding to the outside row of beads, between beads #ef and #eg (purple; Figure 12-17).

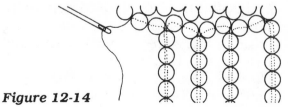

Figure 12-14

90

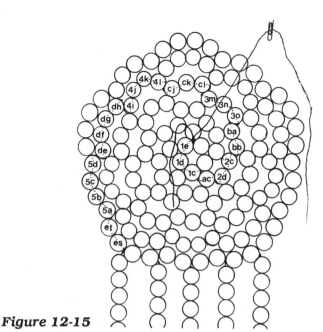

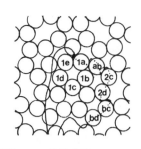

Figure 12-16

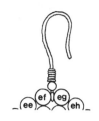

Figure 12-17

Bead Number Pattern: Four Bead Rosette

Figure 12-15

Pattern A: Four Bead Rosette

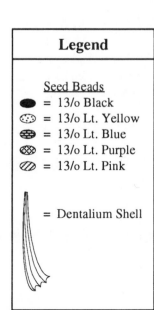

Legend

Seed Beads
- ● = 13/o Black
- ⬭ = 13/o Lt. Yellow
- ⬭ = 13/o Lt. Blue
- ⬭ = 13/o Lt. Purple
- ⬭ = 13/o Lt. Pink

= Dentalium Shell

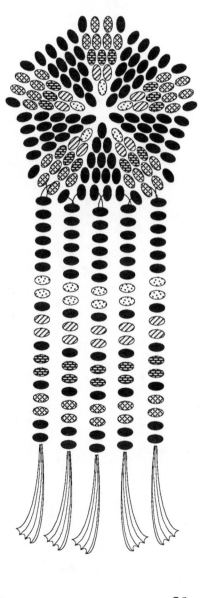

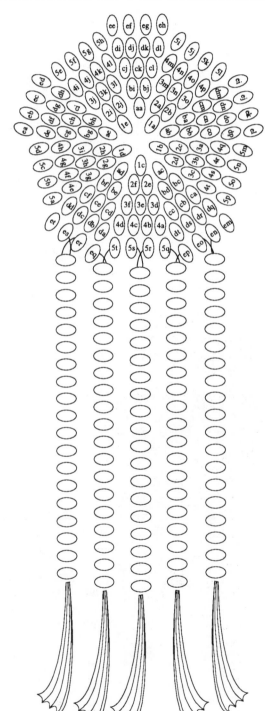

Five-Bead Rosettes - Patterns B to D

These earrings are made with the same technique as the Four-Bead Rosettes. The only difference is that there are five beads per set in rows #5 and #e, which makes for a larger earring. A diagram of the bead number placement for these patterns is again provided. Patterns B to D also provide different color and fringe designs.

Bead Number Pattern: Five Bead Rosette

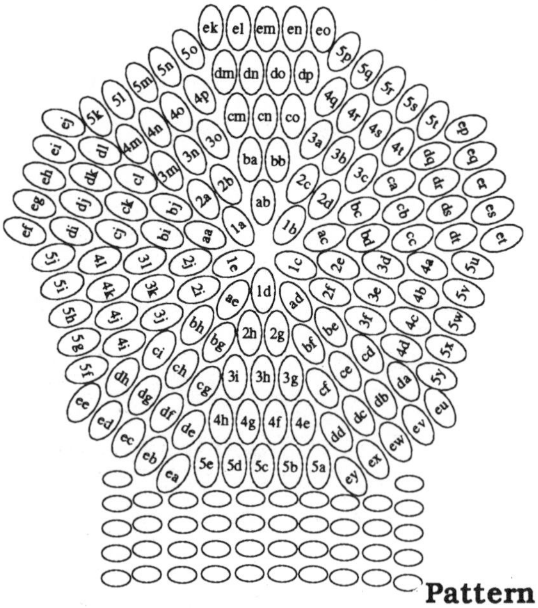

Pattern B: Double Flower

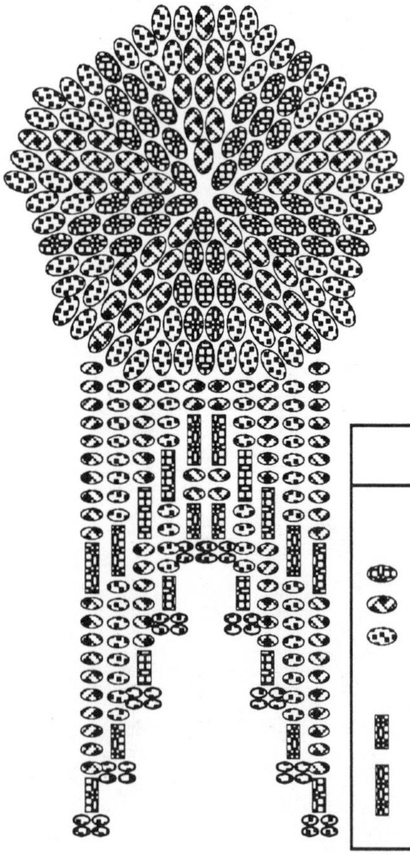

Legend

Seed Beads
= 13/o Med. Red
= 13/o Dk. Purple
= 13/o Dk. Yellow

Bugle Beads
= #3 (7mm) Med. Red
= #5 (11mm) Med. Red

Pattern C: Star

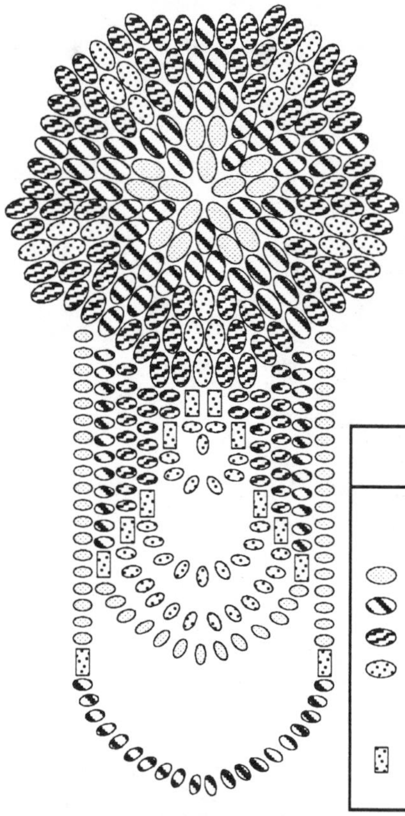

Legend

Seed Beads
= 13/o White
= 13/o Med. Blue
= 13/o Orange
= 13/o Lt. Yellow

Bugle Beads
= #2 (5mm) Lt. Yellow

Pattern D: Arrows

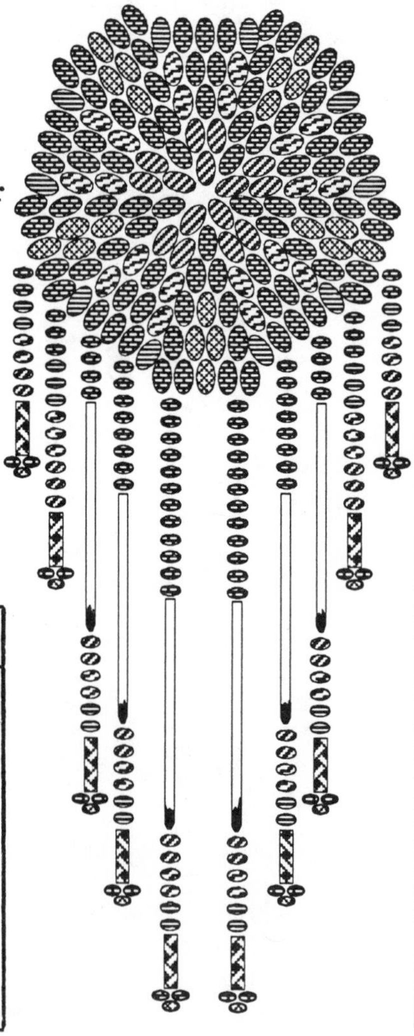

Legend

Seed Beads
= 13/o Dk. Pink
= 13/o Lt. Blue
= 13/o Orange
= 13/o Lt. Purple
= 13/o Peach

Bugle Beads
= 12mm Dk. Purple
= Porcupine Quill

Snowflake Rosette #1 - Pattern E

This earring is a highly modified (and attractive) version of the basic rosette technique. There are six beads in the base row of this earring (instead of five) and after the second row (row #a), the pattern is modified to make the six arms of a snowflake. A bead number diagram is provided.

Bead the first two (base) rows of this earring using the same technique as for the previous rosette earrings. Be sure to follow Pattern E for number and color of beads in each row.

After bead #af has been strung (and the needle has passed through beads #1f and #aa), string bead #2a and push the needle back through bead #aa. Continue through beads #1a and #ab. String another single bead (#2b), go back through bead #ab, and then through beads #1b and #ac (Figure 12-18).

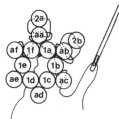

Figure 12-18

Continue adding single beads on top of each bead in row #a, using the technique just described. To end the row, string bead #2f, go down through bead #af and back up through bead #2f (Figure 12-19).

Finish the center section of the earring by making a circle of beads around the two base rows. To start, string three beads in a counterclockwise direction (#ba-#bc) and push the needle through bead #2e. Continue stringing three new beads between each of the beads in row #2 until the circle is complete. The needle and thread should exit out of bead #2f (Figure 12-20).

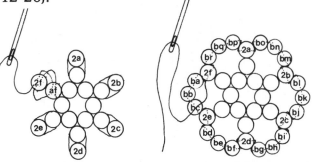

Figure 12-19   *Figure 12-20*

Reinforce the last two rows. To do this, push the needle down through bead #af and back up through bead #2f. Then go through beads #ba-#bc and #2e. Go down through bead #ae and back up through bead #2e. Continue in this manner around the circle, pushing the

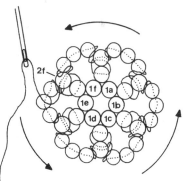

Figure 12-21

needle through the row #b beads and attaching them to the beads in row #2 and row #a, until the needle has passed through bead #2f once again (Figure 12-21). Switch to a size 16 needle at this point (if it has not been necessary by now), because some of the beads ahead already have several threads through them.

To start the snowflake arms (rows #x, #y & #z), string seven beads (#x1-#x7), following the colors in Pattern E. Push the needle counterclockwise through bead #2e. String another seven beads (#x8-#x14) and push the needle through bead #2d. Continue stringing sets of seven beads between the beads in row #2 until six snowflake arms have been strung (Figure 12-22). End by pushing the needle through bead #2f and up through beads #x1-#x4 (Figure 12-23).

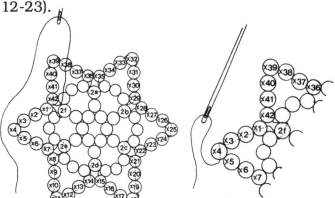

Figure 12-22   *Figure 12-23*

Continue beading the snowflake arms outward with row #y. String beads #y1-#y3 and push the needle down through beads #x4-#x7 and #2e. Go up through beads #x8-#x11 and string the next three beads (#y4-#y6). Push the needle through beads #x11-#x14, #2d, and #x15-#x18. Continue stringing sets of three row #y beads and going through the row #x and row #2 beads as just described, until six new sets of beads have been strung (Figure 12-24).

Push the needle down through beads #x39-#x42 and #2f, then up through beads #x1-#x4 and #y1-#y2. Start the outermost portions of the snowflake arms by stringing beads #z1-#z3. Push the needle down through beads #y2-#y3, #x4-#x7 and #2e. Go up through

93

beads #x8-#x11 and #y4-#y5. String three more beads (#z4-#z6) and push the needle through beads #y5-#y6, #x11-#x14, #2d, #x15-#x18, and #y7-#y8. Continue stringing sets of three new beads, above the row #y beads, until the last set (#z16-#z18) is on the thread (Figure 12-25).

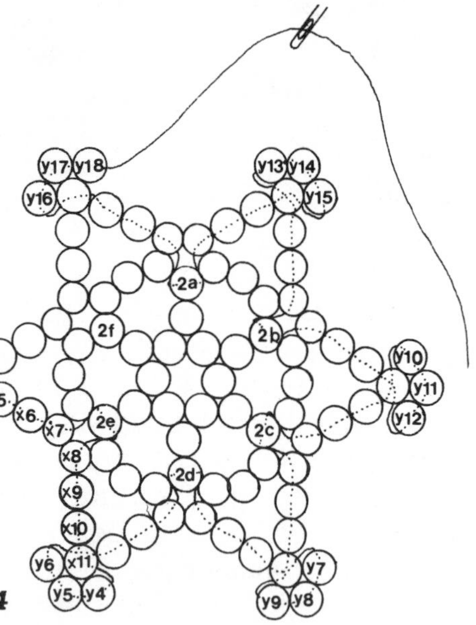

the earring and stiffen it by coating the back side with clear nail polish.

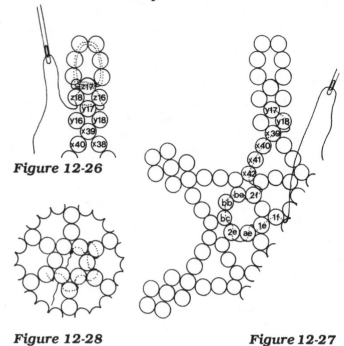

Figure 12-26

Figure 12-24

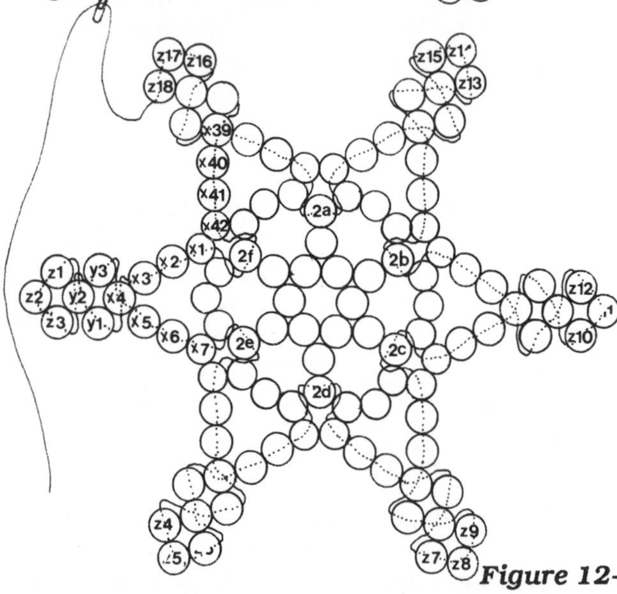

Figure 12-25

Figure 12-28   **Figure 12-27**

Bead Number Pattern: Snowflake #1

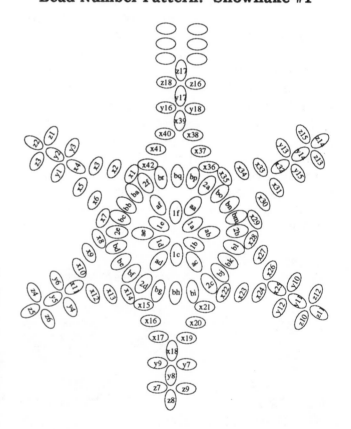

Make the attachment loop of the earring next. Go back through beads #y17, #z16 and #z17. String six loop beads and push the needle back through bead #z17. Go through all the loop beads again and back through beads #z17-#z18 (Figure 12-26).

To finish the earring, work the needle back to the hanging thread, passing through beads #y17-#y18, #x39-#x42, #2f, #ba-#bc, #2e, #ae, and #1e-#1f (Figure 12-27). Knot the main and hanging threads, then hide the ends by weaving them up and down between the two base rows of beads (Figure 12-28). Straighten

94

Pattern E: Snowflake #1

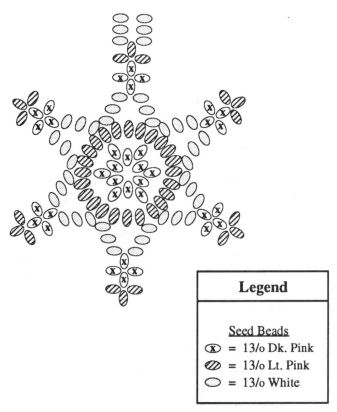

Legend
Seed Beads
⊗ = 13/o Dk. Pink
⊘ = 13/o Lt. Pink
◯ = 13/o White

Snowflake Rosette #2 - Pattern F

Like the previous pattern, there are six beads in the base row of this earring. However, the center portion of Snowflake Rosette #2 is more like the rosettes in Patterns A-D. The earring will tend to buckle at first because of the use of six beads in the base row; however, the design of the earring will compensate for this by the time the snowflake is finished. The design uses 3 mm beads (the aurora borealis finish is prettiest) to accent the seed beads. These are available in plastic or glass (which is heavier) and 12 are required for one pair of earrings.

Thread a size 15 needle with approximately 5 feet of thread. Follow Pattern F and bead the first six rows (through row #c) using the technique described for patterns A-D. Exit out of bead #3b, instead of bead #3c as is normal, at the end of row #c. Refer to the bead placement diagram provided with the pattern for questions about bead number and color.

There are three sets of snowflake arms in this pattern. The first set is attached to the beads in row #3. To start, string three beads (#w1-#w3) and go clockwise through beads #3b and #3c. Continue down through beads #bc-#bd and back up through beads #3d-#3e (Figure 12-29).

String beads #w4-#w6, go back through bead #3e, and then through beads #3f, #be-#bf and #3g-#3h. Continue in this manner, stringing sets of three row #w beads and pushing the needle through the beads in row #3, row #b and back into row #3 as just described, until beads #w16-#w18 have been strung. To end this row, push the needle through beads #3q, #3r, #ba-#bb, #3a-#3b and #w1-#w2 (Figure 12-30).

A ring of six 3 mm beads is now added between the first set of snowflake arms. With the thread coming out out of bead #w2, string the first 3 mm bead and go counterclockwise through bead #w17. String another 3 mm bead and continue to alternate passing through the outer snowflake arm beads and stringing 3 mm beads until a 3 mm bead has been attached between each of the six snowflake arm beads. Push the needle through the first 3 mm bead and through bead #w17 again (Figure 12-31). Pull the thread tight. This creates a raised ring above the rosette base of the earring.

The second set of snowflake arms is attached to the beads in row #c. To start, push the needle clockwise through beads #w18, #3q-#3r and #cp-#cq. String three beads (#x1-#x3), go back through bead #cq, and continue through

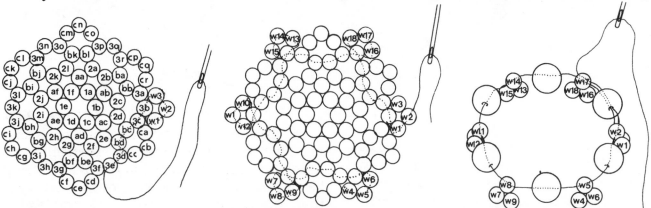

Figure 12-29   **Figure 12-30**   **Figure 12-31**

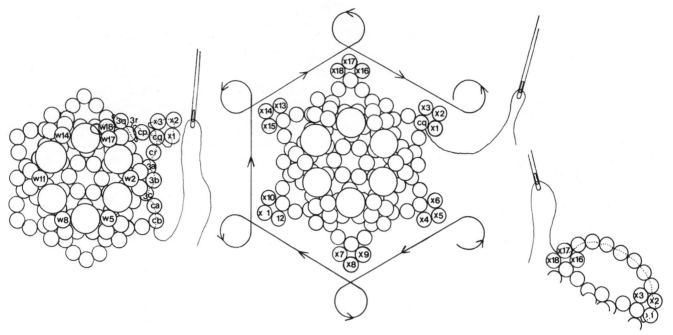

Figure 12-32

Figure 12-33

Figure 12-34

beads #cr, #3a-#3c and #ca-#cb (Figure 12-32). Continue in this manner, stringing sets of three beads above the middle row #c beads until there are six new snowflake arms. The needle should exit out of bead #cq (Figure 12-33).

Next, make an outer ring of beads between the second set of snowflake arms. Push the needle through beads #x1 and #x2, string seven new beads and go counterclockwise through bead #x17 (Figure 12-34). String seven more beads and push the needle through bead #x14. Continue to alternately string seven new beads and pass the thread through the next row #x bead (the top or outer one), until the ring is completed. The needle should exit out of bead #x2. Then push the needle through

the first set of seven beads again and exit out of bead #x17 (Figure 12-35). This creates a flat ring around the rosette base; the remaining snowflake arms are also flat, radiating out from this ring of beads.

To construct the outer portions of the snowflake arms, string three new beads (#y1-#y3). Go back through bead #x17, then go counterclockwise through the next set of seven ring beads and through bead #x14 (Figure 12-36). String beads #y4-#y6, go back through bead #x14, through the next seven ring beads and through bead #x11. Continue in this manner until all six row #x arms have three new beads attached to them. Go through the last set of seven ring beads and exit out of bead #x17 (Figure 12-37).

To complete the outer snowflake arms, first change to a size 16 needle. Then push the needle through beads #y1 and #y2 and string beads #z1-#z3. Go back through bead #y2, then down through beads #y3 and #x17. Continue counterclockwise through the seven

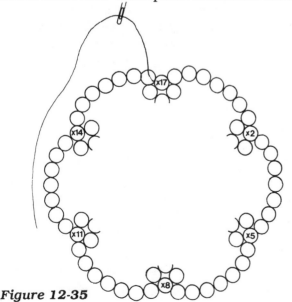

Figure 12-35

Figure 12-36

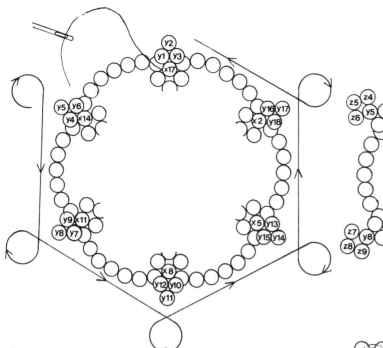

Figure 12-37

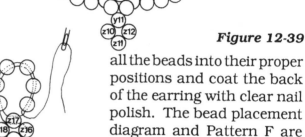

Figure 12-39

outer ring beads and through bead #x14 (Figure 12-38). Go up through beads #y4-#y5. Next, string beads #z4-#z6, go back through bead #y5 and then through beads #y6 and #x14. Continue through the next seven outer ring beads and through beads #x11 and #y7-#y8. Repeat these steps until all six snowflake arms have a set of row #z beads. The needle should exit out of bead #y17 (Figure 12-39).

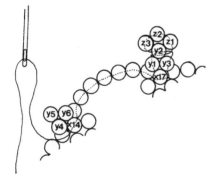

Figure 12-38

Figure 12-40

all the beads into their proper positions and coat the back of the earring with clear nail polish. The bead placement diagram and Pattern F are on the next page.

Make an attachment loop by going up through beads #z16-#z17 and adding six loop beads. Push the needle back through bead #z17 and through all six loop beads again (Figure 12-40).

To complete the earring, work the needle back to the hanging thread by going through beads #z17-#z18, #y17-#y18, #x2-#x3, #cq-#cr, #3a-#3c, #bc-#bd, #2e-#2f, #ad and #1d-#1f. Knot the main and hanging threads together and hide the ends as was done for the basic Rosette Earrings (see Figure 12-16). Push

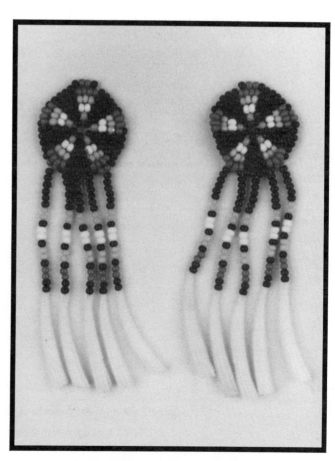

Four Bead Rosette: Pattern A

Bead Number Pattern: Snowflake #2

Pattern F: Snowflake #2

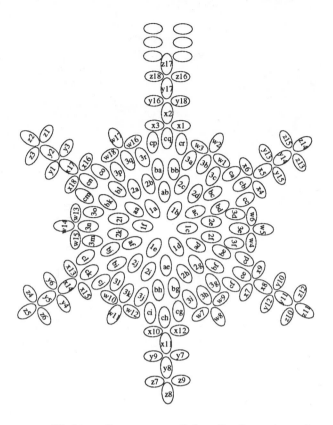

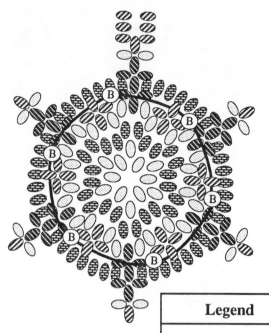

Note: 3mm round beads & outer ring beads omitted for illustrative purposes.

Legend

Seed Beads

⬭ = 13/o White

⬬ = 13/o Lt. Blue

⬭ = 13/o Dk. Pink

⬬ = 13/o Dk. Blue

Ⓑ = 3mm Round Bead (size and actual position altered for illustrative purposes)

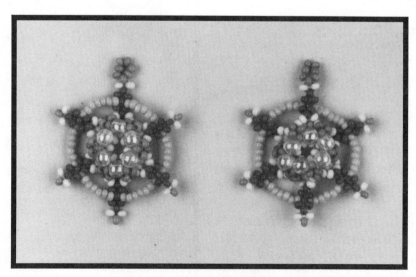

Snowflake Rosette #2: Pattern F

BEADS AND CABOCHONS:
How To Create Fashion Earrings and Jewelry
by
Patricia Lyman

Anyone who enjoys making and wearing their own beautiful earrings will not want to miss this new twist on beaded jewelry. Cabochons are round or oval pieces of precious or semiprecious stone which are domed on top and flat on the back. Surrounded by beads, they make gorgeous pieces of jewelry that everyone will want to own.

Step-by-step, fully illustrated instructions are provided for making earrings, necklaces, barrettes, bolos and brooches. Cabochon Designs include Small Cabochon Button Earrings, Star Rosette Earrings, Star Rosette Brooch, Iridescent Earrings and Necklace, and Starburst Rosette Earrings and Bolo Tie. Brick (or Comanche) Stitch, Peyote Stitch and Applique Designs are also provided in this very versatile book. This is a book that every crafter will want to own and enjoy.

EARRING DESIGNS BY SIG: BOOK I
by
Sigrid Wynne-Evans

Eureka! This book provides the answer to often repeated requests for new and different beading designs and included are some of the best. Both experienced and beginning beaders will cherish this treasure trove of forty-six unique designs all made with the Brick (or Comanche) Stitch technique. The designs will also thrill applique beadworkers who can incorporate these fresh ideas into their projects. Featuring contemporary and Native American themes, the designs focus on pictoral images rather than standard geometric patterns.

This book feaatures complete, illustrated instructions, patterns for each of the projects, and eight pages in full color. Designs include Tropical Fish, Mermaid, Snake, Hummingbird, Dragonfly, Show Girl, Toucan, Beagle, Seahorse, Desert Tapestry, Dragon, Flamingo, Skull, Midnight Coyote, Spirit Dancer, Pegasus, Thunderbird, Peacock, Parrot, Panda, Kokopelli, Polar Bear, Elephant, and more. This book is a must for anyone interested in creating beauty with beads.

EAGLE'S VIEW BESTSELLERS

❑	**Eagle's View Publishing Catalog of Books**	B00/99	$1.50
❑	**The Technique of Porcupine Quill Decoration**/Orchard	B00/01	$8.95
❑	In Hardback	B99/01	$15.95
❑	**The Technique of North American Indian Beadwork**/Smith	B00/02	$10.95
❑	In Hardback	B99/02	$15.95
❑	**Techniques of Beading Earrings** by Deon DeLange	B00/03	$7.95
❑	**More Techniques of Beading Earrings** by Deon DeLange	B00/04	$8.95
❑	**America's *First* First World War: The French & Indian**	B00/05	$8.95
❑	**Crow Indian Beadwork**/Wildschut and Ewers	B00/06	$8.95
❑	**New Adventures in Beading Earrings** by Laura Reid	B00/07	$8.95
❑	**North American Indian Burial Customs** by Dr. H. C. Yarrow	B00/09	$9.95
❑	**Traditional Indian Crafts** by Monte Smith	B00/10	$8.95
❑	**Traditional Indian Bead & Leather Crafts**/ Smith/VanSickle	B00/11	$9.95
❑	**Indian Clothing of the Great Lakes: 1740-1840**/Hartman	B00/12	$9.95
❑	In Hardback	B99/12	$15.95
❑	**Shinin' Trails: A Possibles Bag of Fur Trade Trivia** by Legg	B00/13	$7.95
❑	**Adventures in Creating Earrings** by Laura Reid	B00/14	$9.95
❑	**Circle of Power** by William Higbie	B00/15	$7.95
❑	In Hardback	B99/15	$13.95
❑	**Etienne Provost: Man of the Mountains** by Jack Tykal	B00/16	$9.95
❑	In Hardback	B99/16	$15.95
❑	**A Quillwork Companion** by Jean Heinbuch	B00/17	$9.95
❑	In Hardback	B99/17	$15.95
❑	**Making Indian Bows & Arrows...The Old Way**/Wallentine	B00/18	$9.95
❑	**Making Arrows...The Old Way** by Doug Wallentine	B00/19	$4.00
❑	**Hair of the Bear: Campfire Yarns & Stories** by Eric Bye	B00/20	$9.95
❑	**How To Tan Skins The Indian Way** by Evard Gibby	B00/21	$4.50
❑	**A Beadwork Companion** by Jean Heinbuch	B00/22	$10.95
❑	**Beads and Cabochons** by Patricia Lyman	B00/23	$9.95
❑	**Earring Designs by Sig: Book I** by Sigrid Wynne-Evans	B00/24	$8.95
❑	**Creative Crafts by Marj** by Marj Schneider	B00/25	$9.95
❑	**How To Bead Earrings** by Lori Berry	B00/26	$9.95
❑	**Delightful Beaded Earring Designs** by Jan Radford	B00/27	$8.95
❑	**Earring Designs by Sig: Book II** by Sigrid Wynne-Evans	B00/28	$8.95
❑	**VIDEO - Techniques of Beading Earrings** with Deon DeLange	B00/29	$29.95
❑	**VIDEO - How To Tan Skins The Indian Way** with Evard Gibby	B00/31	$29.95

• •

At your local bookstore or use this handy form for ordering :

EAGLE'S VIEW PUBLISHING READERS SERVICE, DEPT HTBE
6756 North Fork Road - Liberty, Utah 84310

Please send me the above title(s). I am enclosing $_____ (Please add $2.50 per order to cover shipping and handling.) Send check or money order - no cash or C.O.D.s please.

Ms./Mrs./Mr. _____

Address _____

City/State/Zip Code _____

Prices and availability subject to change without notice. Allow three to four weeks for delivery.